Hello! 220 Tequila Recipes

(Tequila Recipes - Volume 1)

Best Tequila Cookbook Ever For Beginners

Ms. Drink

Content

Introduction

***

Hi all,

Welcome to MrandMsCooking.com—a website created by a community of cooking enthusiasts with the goal of providing books for novice cooks featuring the best recipes, at the most affordable prices, and valuable gifts.

Cheers for selecting "Hello! 220 Tequila Recipes" I am confident that my deepest desire to be a writer and my love for beverages will make this article, as well as the others, truly inspiring for you. I treat everyone not only as my followers but also as my friends. With this, as an introduction, I want to impart to you my journey and the reason why I am inspired to create this series. The reason why I love drinking water, or any other beverages is unknown to me, maybe because no chewing is required. I specifically like colored beverages and most of the time, I check the label cautiously before consuming them. This is how my vision to taste a new drink in a different location each day was born. The more I learn about the drink types the more I want to learn. Basically, can be split into these two categories: non-alcoholic and alcoholic. How the drinks are mixed also varies. Two drinks with the same ingredients can taste totally different because two different methods of mixing were used. I began to have more knowledge about drinks and now I am capable of creating my own concoctions the way I want their flavors to be.

Honestly, you do not need to be a genius to create a nice concoction, that's why everyone can definitely do it. If you have a recipe on hand, you can just follow it and change it to fit your preferences. It's that simple!

Moreover, during the summer, beverages are very essential and beneficial. Can you visualize yourself so uncomfortable under the scorching sun? You are only one recipe away from refreshing your soul and easing your discomfort. During those times, I truly cannot think of eating, just drinking. Because I would rather drink only in the summertime, I prefer to create a smoothie containing vegetables (e.g. celery and spinach) and my favorite fruits. Voila! Now, we have something that is both enjoyable and healthy. Just one serving of that beverage can provide me ample energy to do my tasks and to sustain my health.

I was able to create these self-help articles not just because of my undying love for drinks, but also because of I want to impart on my readers my knowledge about different drinks. After years of exploration, I was able to amass all these recipes. Not everyone may like them since we have our own preferences, but I am sure the majority will find something that they will love. Also, don't forget the part where you can tweak these recipes to match your preferences. This article on Drink Recipes shall have two sections:

- Non-alcoholic Recipes
- Alcoholic Recipes

I really appreciate that you have selected "Hello! 220 Tequila Recipes" and for reading to the end. I anticipate that this book shall give you the source of strength during the times that you are really exhausted, as well as be your best friend in the comforts of your own home. Please also give me some love by sharing your own exciting blends in the comments segment below.

List of Abbreviations

C**OO**King LIST OF ABBREVIATIONS	
tbsp(s).	tablespoon(s)
tsp(s).	teaspoon(s)
c.	cup(s)
oz.	ounce(s)
lb(s).	pound(s)

220 Amazing

Tequila Recipes

***

1. A Big, Honkin' Margarita

""This is better than a big margarita.""
Serving: 25 | Prep: 30m | Ready in: 30m

Ingredients

- 5 lemons
- 5 limes
- 3/4 cup white sugar, or to taste
- 1 (750 milliliter) bottle tequila
- 4 cups ice cubes, or as needed

Direction

- Wash limes and lemons. Cut the fruits into quarters. In a 1-gallon glass ice tea jar, squeeze in juices from the fruit quarters and add the squeezed fruit quarters into the jar. Fill ice cubes into the jar. Pour in tequila and sugar. Top the jar with more ice cubes if some of the ice has melted from the tequila. Close the jar and use a wet hand towel, not sopping wet, to wrap the jar.
- Gather about 8 people in a circle and pass the jar from one to the next, each holds the jar and shake it for 3-5 minutes. Once the sugar is dissolved and the hand towel sticks to the jar as it freezes, the drink is ready to serve. Pour the drink into the glasses filled with ice; serve.

Nutrition Information

- Calories: 100 calories;
- Total Carbohydrate: 9.8 g
- Cholesterol: 0 mg
- Total Fat: 0.1 g
- Protein: 0.4 g
- Sodium: 2 mg

2. A Fantastic Margarita

""My husband, who is a bartender, made this one. He likes it when it's garnished with an orange wedge or a lime wedge.""
Serving: 2 | Prep: 3m | Ready in: 3m

Ingredients

- 2 cups limeade prepared from concentrate
- 1/2 cup pineapple juice
- 1/2 cup orange juice
- 2 fluid oz. tequila
- 1 fluid oz. orange liqueur

Direction

- Salt the rims of 2 large margarita glasses into the small plate; pour with salt. Moisten the rims of the glasses by a damp towel and dip them into the salt.
- Mix pineapple juice, orange liqueur, tequila, orange juice, and limeade in a pitcher. Stir well and distribute the mixture into the glasses carefully. Make sure that it won't remove the salt.

3. A Perfect Margarita

"If you happen to have a shaker in your house, then you can practice making this margarita recipe."
Serving: 1 | Prep: 2m | Ready in: 2m

Ingredients

- 1 fluid oz. premium tequila
- 3/4 fluid oz. brandy-based orange liqueur (such as Grand Marnier®)

- 3/4 fluid oz. cointreau
- 3/4 fluid oz. simple syrup
- 1 fluid oz. raspberry flavored liqueur
- 1 lime, juiced
- 1/2 cup sweet and sour mix

Direction

- Drop salt in a small plate to salt the rims of the two margarita glasses. Use a damp towel to moisten the rims of the glasses. Slowly press them into the salt.
- Mix Cointreau, raspberry liqueur, tequila, simple syrup, lime juice, and Grand Marnier in a cocktail mixer filled with ice, about 3/4 full of ice. Stir in sweet and sour until the ice is covered. Shake vigorously and strain the mixture into the glass.

4. Agave Margarita

"One triple sec-free recipe from Tommy's Mexican Restaurant in San Francisco is the inspiration for this recipe."
Serving: Makes 1 serving

Ingredients

- Kosher salt
- 2 lime slices or wedges
- 1/4 cup tequila blanco
- 1 tbsp. agave syrup (nectar)
- 1/4 cup fresh lime juice

Direction

- Pour on a small dish with some kosher salt. Use 1 lime slice to rub over 1/2 the rim of a coupe glass (if you like your Margarita to be up) or an Old-fashioned glass (if you like it to be on the rocks). Dip the glass's rim into salt.
- In a cocktail shaker, combine juice, avage syrup and tequila. Add ice to fill then shake well. In the prepped glass, strain the drink and add another lime slice for garnish.

Nutrition Information

- Calories: 190
- Total Carbohydrate: 17 g
- Total Fat: 0 g
- Fiber: 1 g
- Protein: 0 g
- Sodium: 335 mg
- Saturated Fat: 0 g

5. Aperol-kombucha Cocktail

"A more boozy, more delicious and pretty Aperol spritz."
Serving: 8 servings

Ingredients

- 2 cups gin, tequila, or mezcal
- 1 1/2 cups Aperol
- 1 (16-oz.) bottle chilled kombucha, preferably ginger or lemon flavored
- 4 (12-oz.) cans chilled club soda
- 2 tangerines or oranges, halved through stem ends, thinly sliced

Direction

- In a glass jar or a large pitcher, combine kombucha and Aperol with your chosen spirit. Stir well.
- For cocktail, add ice to fill a small glass. Fill halfway of the glass with gin mixture. Add club soda on top then add 1-2 slices of tangerine slice and a few dashes of bitters to finish.

Nutrition Information

- Calories: 241
- Total Carbohydrate: 14 g
- Total Fat: 0 g
- Fiber: 2 g
- Protein: 1 g
- Sodium: 47 mg
- Saturated Fat: 0 g

6. Austin Margarita (aka Mexican Martini)

"We were finally able to make the perfect margarita. The key is using only fresh fruit juice and do not use any pre-made mixes! Avoid skimping but try to buy juice. To get the best taste, squeeze it by yourself! In case you love olives, you can add pimento stuffed olives. Adding three olives on a stirrer will make your margarita unique."
Serving: 1 | Prep: 15m | Ready in: 15m

Ingredients

- 1/2 cup ice cubes
- 1 (1.5 fluid oz.) jigger silver tequila
- 1 (1.5 fluid oz.) jigger Cointreau
- 2 tsps. Grand Marnier liqueur (optional)
- 2 (1.5 fluid oz.) jiggers freshly squeezed lime juice
- 1 (1.5 fluid oz.) jigger freshly squeezed orange juice
- 1 (1.5 fluid oz.) jigger freshly squeezed lemon juice
- 3 pimento-stuffed green olives (optional)

Direction

- Add ice cubes in a margarita glass. Then add in the Grand Marnier, tequila, and Cointreau. Add in the lemon juice, lime juice, and orange juice to taste. If desired, decorate with a pimento stuffed olive.

7. Bake's Margarita Masterpiece

"This easy to make cocktail can be served with salted rims, garnished with limes if desired."
Serving: 6 | Prep: 10m | Ready in: 10m

Ingredients

- 4 cups ice cubes, or as needed
- 1 (12 oz.) container frozen limeade concentrate
- 6 fluid oz. tequila
- 6 fluid oz. Mexican beer
- 3 fluid oz. triple sec

- 2 fluid oz. melon liqueur (such as Midori®), or to taste

Direction

- Pour ice into a blender; place limeade, melon liqueur, tequila, triple sec, and Mexican beer. Blend until it achieves desired consistency.

Nutrition Information

- Calories: 347 calories;
- Total Carbohydrate: 57.5 g
- Cholesterol: 0 mg
- Total Fat: 0.1 g
- Protein: 0.1 g
- Sodium: 8 mg

8. Baltimore Zoo

"This is an extremely strong beverage. However, you will taste its fruity flavor instead of alcohol. You can alter the amount of orange juice in this drink. Keep in mind that you won't drink this and drive."
Serving: 2 | Prep: 10m | Ready in: 10m

Ingredients

- ice cubes
- 1/2 fluid oz. silver tequila
- 1/2 fluid oz. gin
- 1/2 fluid oz. white rum
- 1/2 fluid oz. vodka
- 1/2 fluid oz. triple sec
- 3 fluid oz. orange juice
- 3 fluid oz. grenadine syrup
- 4 fluid oz. beer (such as Budweiser®)

Direction

- Mix orange juice, vodka, gin, grenadine, triple sec, rum, and tequila in a pitcher filled with ice. Stir in to mix then pour in beer before serving.

Nutrition Information

- Calories: 291 calories;

- Total Carbohydrate: 48 g
- Cholesterol: 0 mg
- Total Fat: 0.1 g
- Protein: 0.6 g
- Sodium: 26 mg

9. Banana Margaritas

"It's a unique version of a known traditional drink. You'll love it!"
Serving: 4 | Prep: 5m | Ready in: 10m

Ingredients

- 6 fluid oz. tequila
- 1 (6 oz.) can frozen limeade concentrate
- 4 fluid oz. triple sec liqueur
- 6 cups ice
- 2 bananas
- 1/4 cup coarse granulated sugar

Direction

- Sugar the rims of 4 large margarita glasses. To do so, drop sugar into a small plate. Wet the rims of the glasses on a damp towel, press them into the sugar.
- Blend triple sec, tequila, limeade, and ice in a blender until smooth. Stir in bananas and blend it again until smooth. Distribute the mixture into the glasses. Serve.

10. Basic Margarita

"You can add your favorite fresh fruits into this basic margarita recipe to flavor it. It's a good choice to use mango or strawberry. You can also substitute margarita salt rims with granulated sugar."
Serving: 4 | Prep: 3m | Ready in: 5m

Ingredients

- 5 fluid oz. tequila
- 3 fluid oz. triple sec
- 2 (6 oz.) cans frozen limeade concentrate
- 4 cups ice cubes
- coarse salt

Direction

- On a small plate, pour the salt; use a damp towel to moisten the rims of 2 large margarita glasses then salt them by pressing into the salt.
- Combine limeade concentrate, triple sec and tequila in a blender. Add ice cubes to fill the blender. Process till smooth. Transfer into glasses and add slice of lime for garnish. Serve.

11. Beer Margaritas

"Margaritas with the flavor of beer. Make sure to use not-so-micro beer brews so it wouldn't overpower the drink. If it's too sweet for you, you can add more water. You can also filter the pulp if you want."
Serving: 6 | Prep: 5m | Ready in: 5m

Ingredients

- 1 (12 fluid oz.) can frozen limeade concentrate
- 12 fluid oz. tequila
- 12 fluid oz. water
- 12 fluid oz. beer
- ice
- 1 lime, cut into wedges

Direction

- In a big pitcher, mix beer, limeade, water, and tequila together until the limeade melts and the mixture is well combined. Put a lot of ice then add lime wedges to garnish. If necessary, pour in more water.

12. Beergarita

*"I knew how to make this from my mother and have loved it
ever since."*
Serving: 12 | Prep: 10m | Ready in: 10m

Ingredients

- 6 (12 fluid oz.) cans or bottles beer
- 1 (12 fluid oz.) can frozen limeade concentrate
  (such as Minute Maid®)
- 12 fluid oz. tequila
- 6 cups ice cubes

Direction

- Into a large pitcher, add the beers. Pour in the
  limeade and stir to mix. Measure out tequila
  with limeade can and then add into the
  pitcher. Stir to combine and then serve atop
  ice.

Nutrition Information

- Calories: 232 calories;
- Total Carbohydrate: 29 g
- Cholesterol: 0 mg
- Total Fat: 0 g
- Protein: 0.8 g
- Sodium: 11 mg

13. Big Kev's Texas Style Long Island Iced Tea

"Party with this Long Island Iced Tea Recipe."
Serving: 1 | Prep: 5m | Ready in: 5m

Ingredients

- 1 fluid oz. vodka
- 1 fluid oz. dry gin
- 1 fluid oz. triple sec (orange-flavored liqueur)
- 1 fluid oz. rum
- 1 fluid oz. tequila
- 1 (12 fluid oz.) can or bottle cola-flavored
  carbonated beverage
- 1 wedge lemon
- 1 wedge lime

Direction

- In an ice-filled tall glass, pour tequila, rum,
  triple sec, gin and vodka. Add cola to top off
  and gently stir. Add lime wedges and lemon
  for garnish.

14. Blackberry Lime Margaritas

Serving: Serves 4.

Ingredients

- 2 cups (about 11 oz.) blackberries
- 2 cups ice cubes
- 1/2 cup fresh lime juice
- 3/4 cup white tequila
- 1/4 cup sugar

Direction

- In a blender, puree the blackberries then force
  in a small bowl through a fine sieve; remove
  the solids. Combine the leftover ingredients
  and 1/2 cup of puree in a cocktail shaker.
  Shake well then strain into 4 stemmed glasses.

Nutrition Information

- Calories: 186
- Total Carbohydrate: 23 g
- Total Fat: 0 g
- Fiber: 4 g
- Protein: 1 g
- Sodium: 7 mg
- Saturated Fat: 0 g

15. Blackberry Margarita

"This recipe is a remake of a restaurant cocktail. It tastes better than the original by far."
Serving: 2 | Prep: 5m | Ready in: 5m

Ingredients

- ice cubes, or as needed
- 1 1/2 (1.5 fluid oz.) jiggers gold tequila
- 2 (1.5 fluid oz.) jiggers sweet and sour mix
- 1/2 lime, juiced
- 1 packet artificial sweetener (such as Splenda®)
- 6 fresh blackberries

Direction

- Put ice in a cocktail shaker until full; add in blackberries, tequila, sweetener, sweet and sour mix, and lime juice. Secure lid and shake.
- Put ice in margarita glasses until full; pour cocktail into glasses.

Nutrition Information

- Calories: 176 calories;
- Total Carbohydrate: 21.2 g
- Cholesterol: 0 mg
- Total Fat: 0.1 g
- Protein: 0.8 g
- Sodium: 5 mg

16. Blackberry-infused Tequila

"Yummy, colorful, and fruity margaritas from a pink liquor."
Serving: 16 | Prep: 15m | Ready in: 14days15m

Ingredients

- 1 cup fresh blackberries
- 1 lime
- 1 (750 milliliter) bottle tequila
- 1/4 cup simple syrup, or to taste (optional)

Direction

- In a 1.5ltr bottle, put in blackberries. Zest lime and add zest to bottle. Take out and discard the connective membranes and the rest of the pith from the lime; only add the remaining pulp in the bottle. Pour in tequila into the bottle.
- Secure lid and place the bottle in a dark and cool area for two weeks. Shake the bottle once a day.
- With a coffee filter or cheesecloth, filter tequila through; mix in simple syrup into the tequila.

Nutrition Information

- Calories: 121 calories;
- Total Carbohydrate: 3.7 g
- Cholesterol: 0 mg
- Total Fat: 0.1 g
- Protein: 0.2 g
- Sodium: < 1 mg

17. Blackberry-mint Julep Margarita

""Top each beverage with a sprig of mint and blackberry. It's so refreshing!""
Serving: 2 | Prep: 5m | Ready in: 5m

Ingredients

- 6 blackberries, plus more for garnish
- 6 leaves fresh mint, plus more for garnish
- 1 oz. bourbon whiskey
- 1 oz. tequila
- 1 oz. lime juice
- 1 tsp. agave nectar
- ice

Direction

- Mix mint and blackberries in a shaker. Stir in lime juice, agave nectar, bourbon, and tequila.
- Add some ice and shake it thoroughly. Strain the mixture into the two julep glasses with fresh ice.

- Calories: 88 calories;
- Total Carbohydrate: 5.3 g
- Cholesterol: 0 mg
- Total Fat: 0.1 g
- Protein: 0.3 g
- Sodium: 4 mg

18. Blue Island Ice Tea

"You'll be knocked down by this Long Island."
Serving: 1 | Prep: 5m | Ready in: 5m

Ingredients

- 1 cup ice cubes
- 1/3 fluid oz. white rum
- 1/3 fluid oz. tequila
- 1/3 fluid oz. gin
- 1/3 fluid oz. blue curacao
- 1/4 fluid oz. vodka
- 1/4 fluid oz. sweet and sour mix
- 1/2 fluid oz. cola
- 1 wedge lime

Direction

- Add ice cubes to fill a highball glass. Pour in cola, sour mix, vodka, blue caracao, gin, tequila and rum. Don't stir and let the layers of liquors remain. Add a lime wedge as garnish to serve.

19. Blue Lagoon Margaritas

"Tasty and gorgeous drink for the summer."
Serving: 1 | Prep: 10m | Ready in: 10m

Ingredients

- 2 fluid oz. sour mix
- 1 1/2 fluid oz. pineapple juice
- 1 1/4 fluid oz. tequila
- 1 fluid oz. Blue Curacao
- 1/2 fluid oz. lime juice
- 1 cup ice, or more if desired

Direction

- In a blender, combine ice, sour mix, lime juice, pineapple juice, Blue Curacao, and tequila until smooth.

Nutrition Information

- Calories: 337 calories;
- Total Carbohydrate: 44.6 g
- Cholesterol: 0 mg
- Total Fat: 0.2 g
- Protein: 0.2 g
- Sodium: 11 mg

20. Blue Meanies

"A slightly sweet twist on the traditional margarita but still packs a punch. This can also be blended with the ice."
Serving: 1 | Prep: 5m | Ready in: 5m

Ingredients

- ice cubes
- 2 fluid oz. tequila (such as Sauza®)
- 1 1/2 fluid oz. orange juice
- 1 fluid oz. triple sec
- 1/2 fluid oz. lemon juice
- 1/2 fluid oz. lime juice
- 1/2 fluid oz. blue Curacao liqueur

Direction

- Add ice cubes to fill a cocktail shaker. Pour blue Curacao, lime juice, lemon juice, triple sec, orange juice and tequila over ice then shake. Strain the drink into an ice-filled pint glass.

Nutrition Information

- Calories: 319 calories;
- Total Carbohydrate: 27.3 g
- Cholesterol: 0 mg
- Total Fat: 0.2 g

- Protein: 0.5 g
- Sodium: 12 mg

21. Blue Motorcycle

"A blue twist with your Long Island Iced Tea."
Serving: 1 | Prep: 2m | Ready in: 2m

Ingredients

- 2 cups ice cubes
- 1/2 (1.5 fluid oz.) jigger vodka
- 1/2 (1.5 fluid oz.) jigger tequila
- 1/2 (1.5 fluid oz.) jigger rum
- 1/2 (1.5 fluid oz.) jigger gin
- 1/2 (1.5 fluid oz.) jigger Blue Curacao
- 1 dash sour mix
- 2 fluid oz. lemon-lime flavored carbonated beverage
- 1 slice fresh lemon

Direction

- Fill the cocktail shaker with ice. Mix the lemon-lime soda, sour mix, Blue Curacao, gin, tum, tequila, and the vodka together. To get a frothy head on the drink, shake vigorously. In a tall bar glass, put the contents of the shaker including the ice in. Use a slice of lemon to garnish.

22. Blue Rita

"This blue cocktail is made with Blue Curacao, sour mix, coconut rum and tequila."
Serving: 1 | Prep: 1m | Ready in: 1m

Ingredients

- 1 1/4 fluid oz. tequila
- 3/4 fluid oz. Blue Curacao
- 1/2 fluid oz. coconut rum
- 4 fluid oz. sour mix
- 1 slice lime wedge

Direction

- Combine sour mix, coconut rum, Blue Curacao and tequila in an ice-filled cocktail mixer. Shake vigorously then strain the drink into the glass. Add a wedge of lime to garnish.

23. Boat Drink

"I was served a drink at a local Mexican restaurant and I decided to recreate it at home. I gave it that name after I figured out how to recreate the drink."
Serving: 1 | Prep: 10m | Ready in: 10m

Ingredients

- 1 (1.5 fluid oz.) jigger good quality silver tequila
- 1/2 (1.5 fluid oz.) jigger melon liqueur (such as Midori®)
- 1/4 (1.5 fluid oz.) jigger triple sec
- 1/2 (1.5 fluid oz.) jigger sour mix
- 1 splash grenadine syrup
- 1 splash lime juice
- 1 (1.5 fluid oz.) jigger orange juice, or to taste
- 1 maraschino cherry for garnish
- 1 wedge orange for garnish

Direction

- Add crushed ice into a margarita glass until filled. Add triple sec, tequila, and melon liqueur into the glass. Then top with orange juice, sour mix, lime juice, and grenadine. Decorate with a wedge of orange and the cherry.

Nutrition Information

- Calories: 341 calories;
- Total Carbohydrate: 46.1 g
- Cholesterol: 0 mg
- Total Fat: 0.3 g
- Protein: 0.5 g
- Sodium: 18 mg

24. Brave Bull

Serving: Serves 1.

Ingredients

- 2 oz. tequila
- 1 oz. Kahlua

Direction

- Fill an Old-fashioned glass almost full with ice cubes then pour in Kahlua and tequila. Stir well.

Nutrition Information

- Calories: 99
- Total Carbohydrate: 4 g
- Total Fat: 1 g
- Fiber: 0 g
- Protein: 0 g
- Sodium: 10 mg
- Saturated Fat: 1 g

25. Bucket Of Margaritas

"You don't need to blend this one! You'll just make these slushy margaritas inside the freezer. Take note to prepare this one ahead of time."
Serving: 6 | Prep: 5m | Ready in: 1day5m

Ingredients

- 4 1/2 cups water
- 1 1/2 cups tequila
- 1 (12 fluid oz.) can frozen limeade
- 1/2 cup triple sec (orange-flavored liqueur)
- 1 whole lime, cut into 6 wedges

Direction

- In a freezer-proof container with a lid, combine the orange liqueur, limeade, water, and tequila; mix. Cover it with its lid. Store it inside the freezer for 24 hours until a slush-like consistency is reached. Pour them in glasses with lime wedges garnished on it.

26. Bulldog Margarita

"An easy-to-make bulldog margarita."
Serving: 2 | Prep: 10m | Ready in: 10m

Ingredients

- ice
- 1 cup tequila
- 1 (8 oz.) can frozen limeade concentrate
- 1/2 cup triple sec
- 2 (12 oz.) bottles Mexican beer (such as Corona®)

Direction

- Add ice to fill 3/4 of a blender. Pour in triple sec, limeade concentrate and tequila. Process till ice is broken down into a slushy consistency.
- Transfer the mixture to a 24-oz. margarita glass. Place the beer bottles upside down in the mixture and lean against the glass's rim.

Nutrition Information

- Calories: 921 calories;
- Total Carbohydrate: 111.5 g
- Cholesterol: 0 mg
- Total Fat: 0.2 g
- Protein: 1.7 g
- Sodium: 23 mg

27. Café Iguana Margarita

"This recipe comes from Denver, Colorado."
Serving: 12 Servings

Ingredients

- Lime wedges
- Coarse salt
- 3 1/2 cups Homemade Sweet-and-Sour Mix for Margaritas (click for recipe)
- 1 cup gold tequila

- 1/2 cup Triple Sec
- 16 ice cubes
- 12 lime slices

Direction

- Use lime wedges to rub the rims of 12 glasses then let the rims dip in coarse salt.
- In a blender, combine 8 ice cubes, 1/4 cup of Triple Sec, 1/2 cup of tequila and 1 3/4 cups of sweet-and-sour mix. Process to blend well. Transfer the mixture into 6 glasses. Do the same with the leftover ice cubes, Triple Sec, tequila and sweet-and-sour mix. Transfer into 6 glasses and add a lime slice to each glass for garnish.

28. Cancun Martini

"This combination of coffee liqueur and tequila will bring you an unbelievable and not-too-sweet exotic flavor."
Serving: 1 | Prep: 5m | Ready in: 5m

Ingredients

- 1 (1.5 fluid oz.) jigger tequila (such as Jose Cuervo®)
- 1/2 fluid oz. coffee-flavored liqueur (such as Trader Vic's®)
- 1 maraschino cherry

Direction

- Fill a shaker with ice and add in coffee-flavored liqueur and tequila. Cover and shake till it's chilled. Into a martini glass, strain the drink then use a maraschino cherry to garnish.

Nutrition Information

- Calories: 158 calories;
- Total Carbohydrate: 7.6 g
- Cholesterol: 0 mg
- Total Fat: 0.1 g
- Protein: 0 g
- Sodium: 2 mg

29. Chipotle Sangrita

"You need to puree some of the chipotle peppers in adobo sauce for this recipe."

Ingredients

- 1 cup tomato juice
- 1 tsp. chipotle puree in adobo sauce
- Juice from 1 lemon wedge
- 1 1/2-oz. chilled shot of reposado tequila

Direction

- Combine lemon juice, chipotle puree and tomato juice. Stir well and let chill. Once ready to serve, pour the mixture alongside with the chilled shot of reposado tequila into a shot glass. Shoot the tequila shot then follow with the shot of Sangrita.

Nutrition Information

- Calories: 71
- Total Carbohydrate: 5 g
- Total Fat: 0 g
- Fiber: 1 g
- Protein: 1 g
- Sodium: 40 mg
- Saturated Fat: 0 g

30. Cider And Tequila Hot Toddy

Serving: Makes about 6 cups

Ingredients

- 4 cups apple cider
- 1 cup cranberry juice cocktail
- 1/2 cup tequila
- 1/4 cup Triple Sec or other orange-flavored liqueur
- Garnish: lime slices

Direction

- Heat cranberry juice cocktail and heat cider in a saucepan till hot; don't boil. Take away from the heat. Add in liqueurs and tequila. Place toddies in mugs to serve and add lime slices to garnish.

Nutrition Information

- Calories: 271
- Total Carbohydrate: 45 g
- Total Fat: 0 g
- Fiber: 0 g
- Protein: 0 g
- Sodium: 13 mg
- Saturated Fat: 0 g

---

31. Clamato® Vampirito

"This steamy drink of tequila and Clamato® will satisfy your nocturnal instincts."
Serving: 1 | Prep: 5m | Ready in: 5m

Ingredients

- 3 slices fresh lime
- 5 fresh basil leaves
- 1 dash habanero pepper sauce, or to taste
- 4 oz. Clamato® Tomato Cocktail
- 1 1/2 oz. tequila (optional)
- 2 oz. Squirt® citrus soda
- 1 lime wheel
- Ice, as needed

Direction

- Combine all the ingredients in a shaker, except lime slices and Squirt(R) Citrus soda. Shake well till chilled. Strain into ice-filled glass. Add Squirt soda to fill. Add lime wheel for garnish.

Nutrition Information

- Calories: 161 calories;
- Total Carbohydrate: 15.6 g
- Cholesterol: 0 mg
- Total Fat: 0.1 g

- Protein: 0.8 g
- Sodium: 439 mg

---

32. Classic Frozen Strawberry Margarita

"A new spin to a traditional frozen margarita!"
Serving: 1 | Prep: 10m | Ready in: 10m

Ingredients

- 1/4 cup sliced fresh strawberries
- 1 1/2 fluid oz. tequila
- 1 fluid oz. lime juice
- 1/2 fluid oz. triple sec
- 1 tsp. white sugar, or to taste
- 1 cup ice cubes
- 1 wedge lime (optional)
- 1 tsp. white sugar (optional)

Direction

- Use a blender to mix the triple sec, lime juice, strawberries, 1 tsp. of sugar and tequila together for about 10 seconds. Put in the ice cubes then run the blender on high setting for about 15 seconds until the ice has been crushed.
- Run a wedge of lime around the glass rim. Put 1 tsp. of sugar scattered evenly on a plate. Dip the rim of the glass onto the sugar to coat the rim. Put the prepared margarita mix into the prepared glass.

Nutrition Information

- Calories: 206 calories;
- Total Carbohydrate: 21.3 g
- Cholesterol: 0 mg
- Total Fat: 0.2 g
- Protein: 0.4 g
- Sodium: 10 mg

33. Classic Shaken Margaritas

"Persian limes aren't as sweet as Key and Mexican limes."
Serving: Serves 2

Ingredients

- 1 lime, cut crosswise into 5 slices
- Coarse salt
- 1 cup ice cubes
- 1/2 cup premium tequila
- 1/4 cup triple sec or other orange liqueur
- 2 tbsps. fresh lime juice

Direction

- Place a single layer consists of 3 lime slices on a small plate. On a separated small plate, add enough salt to reach 1/4-in. deep. Press lime slices lightly on 2 Margarita glasses' rims, twist till juices are extracted and rims are coated. Lightly coat the moistened rims by dipping them into salt.
- In a cocktail shaker, combine lime juice, triple sec, tequila and ice cubes. Shake till it's frosty on the outside of the shaker. In the prepped glasses, strain the mixture and add the 2 leftover lime slices to garnish the rims. Serve immediately.

Nutrition Information

- Calories: 250
- Total Carbohydrate: 16 g
- Total Fat: 0 g
- Fiber: 1 g
- Protein: 0 g
- Sodium: 600 mg
- Saturated Fat: 0 g

34. Coco Loco

"You can use gin or banana liqueur instead of the melon liqueur."
Serving: 1 | Prep: 15m | Ready in: 15m

Ingredients

- 1 fresh coconut
- 1 cup ice
- 1 fluid oz. white tequila
- 1 fluid oz. melon liqueur
- 1 fluid oz. coconut rum
- 1 fluid oz. pineapple juice
- 1 fluid oz. sugar syrup
- 1/2 fresh lime

Direction

- To make a coconut tumbler: carefully cut off 2 inches on the top of the coconut, reserve the coconut milk inside. Place into the coconut's cavity with sugar syrup, pineapple juice, rum, melon liqueur, tequila and ice. Squeeze over the mixture with the lime half and let the lime drop into the drink. Stir.

35. Coco Lopo

"You can find this coconut blended drink in many restaurants."
Serving: 8 | Prep: 5m | Ready in: 5m

Ingredients

- 1 cup gin
- 1 cup 151 proof rum
- 1 cup vodka
- 1 cup tequila
- 1 cup grenadine syrup
- 1 (8 oz.) can cream of coconut

Direction

- Into a blender, add the cream of coconut, gin, vodka, rum, grenadine, and tequila. Add ice and then blend until smooth.

36. Coconut Margarita

"A mildly sweet margarita that everyone will surely love! Don't use sweet and sour mixes with synthetic ingredients because they don't taste really good. You may serve it in toasted coconut flake-rimmed glasses if you want. Pour it over ice and drink to your heart's content!"
Serving: 8 | Prep: 10m | Ready in: 10m

Ingredients

- 2 cups sweet and sour mix (such as Bone Daddy®)
- 1 cup tequila (such as Cuervo Gold®)
- 1/2 cup triple sec liqueur
- 1/2 cup coconut milk
- 2 limes, juiced

Direction

- In a pitcher, vigorously stir the coconut milk, sweet and sour mix, lime juice, tequila and triple sec together to blend. Pour the cocktail mix over ice and serve.

Nutrition Information

- Calories: 272 calories;
- Total Carbohydrate: 32.2 g
- Cholesterol: 0 mg
- Total Fat: 3.1 g
- Protein: 0.3 g
- Sodium: 3 mg

37. Coconut Margaritas

"Enjoy the coconut margaritas like the one in Costa Rica!"
Serving: 4 | Prep: 10m | Ready in: 10m

Ingredients

- 2 cups ice
- 3/4 cup sweetened coconut cream
- 4 1/2 fluid oz. tequila
- 1 1/2 fluid oz. triple sec
- 1/4 cup sweetened flaked coconut

Direction

- In a blender place ice; pour the coconut cream, triple, sec, and tequila to blend until smooth at high speed. On a plate, scatter the coconut. Take the rims of four glasses to wet. In the coconut, dip the glass rims. Take the margaritas to the prepared glasses.

38. Coronarita

"A cheeky margarita-type drink. Use the pitcher to prepare it and you can easily increase it. Perfect when relaxing in the sun or on a hot summer day for a barbeque!"
Serving: 6 | Prep: 10m | Ready in: 10m

Ingredients

- 2 (12 fluid oz.) cans or bottles lemon-lime soda, or more to taste
- 1 (12 oz.) bottle Mexican beer (such as Corona®)
- 1 (12 fluid oz.) can frozen limeade concentrate
- 12 fluid oz. tequila
- ice
- 2 leaves mint, chopped, or more to taste (optional)

Direction

- Into a large pitcher, add frozen limeade, lemon-lime soda, and Mexican beer. Measure out tequila with an empty limeade can and then add into the pitcher. Stir thoroughly to combine. Serve atop ice decorated with chopped mint.

Nutrition Information

- Calories: 386 calories;
- Total Carbohydrate: 60.3 g
- Cholesterol: 0 mg
- Total Fat: 0 g
- Protein: 0.3 g
- Sodium: 19 mg

39. Cowboy Margaritas

"This drink has the perfect balance of tang, sweet, and tart. Best enjoyed on the rocks or frozen in a glass with sugar on the rim."
Serving: 6 | Prep: 10m | Ready in: 10m

Ingredients

- 1 (12 oz.) container frozen limeade concentrate
- 6 fluid oz. tequila
- 3 fluid oz. raspberry-flavored liqueur
- 1 (12 fluid oz.) can or bottle light beer

Direction

- In a blender, mix raspberry-flavored liqueur, tequila, and limeade together until well combined. Mix in it the light beer gradually.

Nutrition Information

- Calories: 316 calories;
- Total Carbohydrate: 53 g
- Cholesterol: 0 mg
- Total Fat: 0 g
- Protein: 0.1 g
- Sodium: 4 mg

40. Crazy Casey's Long Island Spiced Tea

"This recipe adds a little more island spice to a traditional Long Island."
Serving: 1 | Prep: 10m | Ready in: 10m

Ingredients

- 4 tsps. white sugar
- 4 tbsps. water
- 4 tsps. fresh lime juice
- 4 tsps. fresh lemon juice
- 1 fluid oz. spiced rum
- 1 fluid oz. tequila
- 1 fluid oz. vodka
- 1 fluid oz. gin
- 1 fluid oz. triple sec (orange-flavored liqueur)
- 1 cup ice cubes
- 2 fluid oz. cola-flavored carbonated beverage
- 1 lemon wedge

Direction

- In a glass, stir together triple sec, gin, vodka, tequila, rum, lemon juice, lime juice, water and sugar till the sugar dissolves. Place in ice and add in the cola. Add the lemon wedge for garnish and serve.

41. Creamy Coconut Margarita

""Here's a refreshing and delicious cross between pina colada and margarita.""
Serving: 6 | Prep: 10m | Ready in: 10m

Ingredients

- 1 (15 oz.) can cream of coconut (such as Coco Lopez®)
- 1 cup ice
- 3/4 cup tequila (such as Sauza® 100% Blue Agave)
- 1/2 cup freshly squeezed lime juice
- 1/4 cup brandy-based orange liqueur (such as Grand Marnier®)

Direction

- In a blender, blend the orange liqueur, cream of coconut, lime juice, ice, and tequila until smooth.

Nutrition Information

- Calories: 379 calories;
- Total Carbohydrate: 48.4 g
- Cholesterol: 0 mg
- Total Fat: 12.6 g
- Protein: 0.1 g
- Sodium: 40 mg

42. Cucumber-celery Margarita

Serving: Makes 1

Ingredients

- Kosher salt
- 4 cucumber slices
- 2 oz. tequila
- 1 oz. fresh lime juice
- 3/4 oz. agave syrup (nectar)
- 4 dashes of celery shrub

Direction

- Rub lime and coat kosher salt onto 1/2 of the rim of a Collins glass. In a cocktail shaker, muddle 4 cucumber slices then add 4 dashes of celery shrub, 3/4 oz. of avage syrup or nectar, 1 oz. of fresh lime juice and 2 oz. of tequila; fill in ice cubes. Cover then shake till it's frosty on the outside of the shaker. Transfer into prepped glasses.

Nutrition Information

- Calories: 208
- Total Carbohydrate: 20 g
- Total Fat: 0 g
- Fiber: 0 g
- Protein: 0 g
- Sodium: 324 mg
- Saturated Fat: 0 g

43. D.i.y. Drinks Bar

Ingredients

- In bowls, put out diced pineapple, mango, watermelon, kiwi, lemon, lime, orange, and grapefruit; raspberries, blueberries, and diced strawberries; mint and basil. Arrange spiced syrups, sparkling water, crushed ice, measuring spoons, muddlers, vodka, gin, rum, and tequila on the table.

Direction

- In a glass, place some herb leaves, 1 tbsp. of citrus fruit and 2 tbsp. of diced fruit.
- Use a muddler or spoon to crush.
- To taste or add 2 tbsp. of syrup.
- Add crushed ice to fill the glass.
- Add in spirits and mix.
- Add club soda or sparkling water on top.
- Best combinations
- Vodka, citrus syrup, mint, lemon, pineapple
- Gin, ginger syrup, lime, mango
- Rum, orange, watermelon
- Tequila, grapefruit, kiwi

44. Dane's Frozen Peach Margaritas

"You should prepare margarita during peach season. Decorate with lime slice and peach slice."
Serving: 3 | Prep: 10m | Ready in: 10m

Ingredients

- 2 cups ice cubes, or as desired
- 1 fresh peach, pitted and sliced
- 2 1/2 (1.5 fluid oz.) jiggers tequila
- 1 (1.5 fluid oz.) jigger triple sec
- 1 (1.5 fluid oz.) jigger peach schnapps
- 1 lime, juiced
- 1 tbsp. agave nectar

Direction

- In a blender, blend together peach schnapps, ice cubes, peach, agave nectar, tequila, lime juice, and triple sec for approximately 30 seconds until smooth.

Nutrition Information

- Calories: 218 calories;
- Total Carbohydrate: 21.7 g
- Cholesterol: 0 mg
- Total Fat: 0.1 g
- Protein: 0.1 g
- Sodium: 9 mg

45. Dr. Horrible

"A very potent drink but the punch of the tequila will be cut off by the sweetness from the Kahlua® cuts. It should be sipped very slowly."
Serving: 1 | Prep: 5m | Ready in: 5m

Ingredients

- 1/2 cup ice cubes, or as needed
- 1 (1.5 fluid oz.) jigger tequila
- 1/2 (1.5 fluid oz.) jigger Puerto Rican rum
- 1/2 (1.5 fluid oz.) jigger coffee-flavored liqueur (such as Kahlua®)

Direction

- Add ice to fill a cocktail shaker. Add coffee-flavored liqueur, rum and tequila. Cover and shake. In a glass, strain the drink.

Nutrition Information

- Calories: 225 calories;
- Total Carbohydrate: 8.4 g
- Cholesterol: 0 mg
- Total Fat: 0.1 g
- Protein: 0 g
- Sodium: 6 mg

46. Easy 4-ingredient Margarita

"Start the party with this refreshing and easy-to-make margarita. Serve in a salt-rimmed glass and top with cilantro."
Serving: 1 | Prep: 5m | Ready in: 5m

Ingredients

- 1 cup ice cubes, or as needed
- 1/3 cup tequila
- 1/3 cup agave nectar
- 1 lime, juiced
- 1/2 lemon, juiced

Direction

- Put ice in a cocktail shaker until full; add in lemon juice, tequila, lime juice, and agave nectar. Cover the cocktail shaker and shake well. Transfer margarita into a glass.

Nutrition Information

- Calories: 504 calories;
- Total Carbohydrate: 88.5 g
- Cholesterol: 0 mg
- Total Fat: 0 g
- Protein: 0.2 g
- Sodium: 9 mg

47. Easy Frozen Margaritas

"Margaritas are usually time-consuming to prepare and have very expensive ingredients. Thankfully I discovered a shortcut and easy process in making one. Try using frozen limeade. If ever you're making a non-alcoholic drink, mix a 48-oz. bottle of sparkling water and a thawed 12-oz. can of limeade."
Serving: 8

Ingredients

- 2 quarts ice cubes
- 1 (12 fluid oz.) can frozen limeade concentrate
- 12 fluid oz. tequila (measure with empty limeade can)
- 1/4 cup Cointreau
- Garnish:
- margarita or kosher salt for the rims
- lime slices cut in half

Direction

- In a blender, working in 2 batches, place 1 quart of ice cubes. Drizzle 2 tbsp. of Cointreau, 6-oz. of tequila, and a half can of limeade. Set the blender's speed to the high and blend until the drink is almost smooth. Transfer into a pitcher. Do the same with the remaining ingredients and store them inside the freezer.

- Add a single layer of salt in a salad plate to salt the margarita glasses. Use lime to moisten the rims of each margarita glass. Transfer the margaritas into each glasses and garnish each with lime. Serve immediately.

48. Framboise Fizz

"This refreshing tequila-based cocktail has a sweet finish from the framboise (raspberry liqueur)."
Serving: 1 | Prep: 5m | Ready in: 5m

Ingredients

- 1 1/2 fluid oz. tequila
- 3/4 fluid oz. white creme de cacao
- 3/4 fluid oz. lemon juice
- 1 cup ice cubes
- 2 fluid oz. framboise
- 3 fresh raspberries

Direction

- In a cocktail shaker, combine lemon juice, creme de cacao and tequila. Place in ice, cover then shake till chilled. In a chilled cocktail glass, strain the drink and top off with framboise.
- Add 3 raspberries on a toothpick for garnish.

Nutrition Information

- Calories: 286 calories;
- Total Carbohydrate: 25.7 g
- Cholesterol: 0 mg
- Total Fat: 0 g
- Protein: 0.4 g
- Sodium: 10 mg

49. Frozen Avocado Margaritas

"Smooth and sweet margaritas featuring avocados."
Serving: 4 | Prep: 10m | Ready in: 10m

Ingredients

- 2 cups crushed ice
- 6 fluid oz. tequila
- 4 fluid oz. lime juice
- 2 fluid oz. triple sec
- 1 avocado - peeled, pitted and diced
- 1 sprig fresh cilantro
- coarse salt to taste

Direction

- Blend cilantro, ice, avocado, tequila, Triple Sec, and lime juice in a blender until smooth. Serve on salt-rimmed glasses.

50. Frozen Banana Margaritas

""We have been endeavoring to copy the banana margaritas of Mexico ever since we tasted it. Now it's here! Best when served in sugar or salt-rimmed margarita glasses.""
Serving: 8 | Prep: 15m | Ready in: 15m

Ingredients

- 2 tbsps. lemon juice
- 2 tbsps. lime juice
- 3/4 cup banana liqueur
- 1/2 cup tequila
- 1/4 cup triple sec (orange-flavored liqueur)
- 6 ice cubes
- 2 large bananas

Direction

- Fill the container of a blender with lemon juice, tequila, triple sec, banana liqueur, bananas, lime juice, and add ice cubes so that the mixture will reach up to the 6 cup line. Cover and blend the mixture until smooth. Distribute the mixture among the margarita glasses. Serve.

51. Frozen Honeydew Margaritas

Serving: Serves 4.

Ingredients

- 1 honeydew melon
- 3/4 cup white tequila
- 1/3 cup fresh lime juice
- 2 1/2 tbsp. sugar, or to taste

Direction

- Discard and remove seeds and rind from the melon. Chop enough fruit into 1/2-in. cubes to get 3 1/2 cups. Place melon cubes in a sealable plastic bag and freeze for at least 3 hours and no more than 1 week.
- In a blender, puree the leftover ingredients with frozen honeydew till smooth. Transfer the drink to 4 stemmed glasses.

Nutrition Information

- Calories: 222
- Total Carbohydrate: 32 g
- Total Fat: 0 g
- Fiber: 2 g
- Protein: 1 g
- Sodium: 46 mg
- Saturated Fat: 0 g

52. Frozen Limes Filled With Sangrita And Tequila

"A spicy and salty juice mixture. Just pour the tequila and sangrita into shot glasses if the frozen lime cups can't be prepared in time. Combine the sangrita with a reposado tequila for a richer impact, a smoother sip and more complex flavor."
Serving: Serves 12

Ingredients

- 12 limes, ends trimmed, cut crosswise in half
- 2 1/4 cups fresh orange juice
- 5 tbsps. grenadine syrup
- 1 tsp. (generous) salt
- 1 tsp. cayenne pepper
- Premium tequila

Direction

- Use a citrus juicer to squeeze lime halves and extract as much juice as you can. Pour 3/4 cup of lime juice in a bowl; let chill, covered. Save up the leftover juice for use later. Use a scissors to cut out membranes from the lime halves that have been hollowed. Place lime cups in a resealable plastic bag and seal. Store in the freezer for 4 hours.
- In a blender, mix cayenne, salt, grenadine, 3/4 cup of lime juice and orange juice. Place the mixture into the pitcher. Store the sangrita in the fridge, covered for 2 hours till cold. You can make this the day before. Make sure the sangrita is chilled and the lime cups are frozen.
- Place frozen lime cups on a serving tray. Fill 12 lime cups with the sangrita and fill the leftover 12 lime cups with tequila. Serve immediately.

53. Frozen Margarita

"This classic frozen margarita can be an adult refreshing slushy."
Serving: Serves 1

Ingredients

- 1 jigger (1 1/2 oz.) tequila
- 1 jigger (1 1/2 oz.) fresh lime juice
- 1/2 tsp. superfine granulated sugar
- 1 pony (1 oz.) Triple Sec or Cointreau
- 5 ice cubes

Direction

- Use a cut lime to rub an old-fashioned glass's rim then coat it lightly by dipping it in the salt. Let the glass chill. Blend ice cubes and the

ingredients in a blender for 30 seconds.
Transfer into the glass.

---

54. Frozen Melon Margaritas

""It's the easiest recipe of a tangy and delicious frozen margarita.""
Serving: 8 | Prep: 10m | Ready in: 10m

Ingredients

- 4 cups ice cubes
- 1 (12 oz.) can frozen limeade concentrate
- 2/3 cup tequila
- 1/2 cup melon-flavored schnapps

Direction

- In a blender, blend the melon-flavored schnapps, limeade, tequila, and ice until smooth.

Nutrition Information

- Calories: 235 calories;
- Total Carbohydrate: 41.1 g
- Cholesterol: 0 mg
- Total Fat: 0 g
- Protein: 0 g
- Sodium: 5 mg

---

55. Frozen Raspberry Margaritas

"The orange juice-mint-and-frozen raspberries combo makes this drink an absolute must-try!"
Serving: 6 | Prep: 10m | Ready in: 10m

Ingredients

- 1 cup frozen unsweetened raspberries
- 3/4 cup gold tequila
- 3/4 cup fresh orange juice
- 1/2 cup fresh lemon juice
- 1/4 cup brandy-based orange liqueur (such as Grand Marnier®)
- 2 tbsps. superfine sugar
- 4 mint leaves
- 4 ice cubes

Direction

- Use a blender to mix the lemon juice, mint leaves, tequila, orange liqueur, superfine sugar, orange juice and raspberries together until mixture is smooth in consistency. Put in the ice cubes, one by one, crushing each cube before adding another ice to the blender. Transfer the cocktail mixture into chilled cocktail glasses then serve.

Nutrition Information

- Calories: 176 calories;
- Total Carbohydrate: 24.1 g
- Cholesterol: 0 mg
- Total Fat: 0.2 g
- Protein: 0.6 g
- Sodium: 2 mg

---

56. Frozen Raspberry-ginger Margarita

"This margarita has a sweet-tart flavor of frozen raspberries. This drink also got its spiciness from the fresh ginger."
Serving: Makes 4 | Prep: 15m

Ingredients

- 3 cups frozen raspberries
- 1 cup tequila blanco
- 3/4 cup fresh lime juice
- 1/4 cup agave syrup
- 1 1/2 tsps. finely grated ginger
- 4 (1/4-inch-thick) lime wheels (optional)
- Kosher salt (optional)

Direction

- In a blender, blend the tequila, agave, 2 cups of ice, lime juice, ginger, and raspberries until smooth.

- Use lime to rub the rims of old-fashioned or rock glasses, if desired. Dip the rims into the salt. Divide the cocktail among the prepared glasses. If desired, serve them with lime wheels.

Nutrition Information

- Calories: 238
- Total Carbohydrate: 27 g
- Total Fat: 1 g
- Fiber: 7 g
- Protein: 1 g
- Sodium: 3 mg
- Saturated Fat: 0 g

57. Frozen Strawberry Margarita

"This recipe will surely liven up a party."
Serving: 4 | Prep: 10m | Ready in: 10m

Ingredients

- 6 fluid oz. tequila
- 2 fluid oz. triple sec
- 8 oz. frozen strawberries
- 4 fluid oz. frozen limeade concentrate
- 6 cups ice

Direction

- Crush ice for 15-20 seconds in a blender. Blend in limeade, triple sec, tequila and frozen strawberries till smooth.

58. Frozen Strawberry Margarita Pie

"It's easy to put together this mildly spiked dessert and it'll soon be your summer-entertaining standbys."
Serving: Makes 8 servings | Prep: 40m

Ingredients

- 1 1/4 cups graham cracker crumbs from 9 (2 1/4- by 4 3/4-inch) crackers
- 2 tbsps. sugar
- 5 tbsps. unsalted butter, melted
- 1 lb strawberries, halved (3 1/2 cups)
- 1 tbsp. finely grated fresh lime zest (from 3 limes)
- 1/4 cup fresh lime juice (from 2 limes)
- 1 (14-oz) can sweetened condensed milk
- 2 tbsps. tequila
- 2 tbsps. triple sec, Cointreau, or other orange-flavored liqueur
- 1 1/2 cups chilled heavy cream
- Garnish: small strawberries

Direction

- For crust: Preheat the oven to 350°F with the rack in the middle.
- In a bowl, use a fork to stir together butter, sugar and graham cracker crumbs till well combined. On a buttered 9-in. glass or metal pie plate with the capacity of 4 cups, press the mixture onto the bottom and up the side.
- Bake for 10 minutes then place on a rack for 30 minutes to let cook in pie plate.
- For filling: In a blender, purée liqueur, tequila, condensed milk, lime juice, zest and strawberries till just smooth. Place on a large bowl.
- In a separate bowl, use an electric mixer to beat cream at medium speed till stiff peaks just form. Gently but thoroughly fold into the strawberry mixture with 1/3 of cream to lighten. In 2 batches, fold in the leftovers.
- Transfer the filling to the crust and slightly mound. Uncover and store in the freezer for 4 hours till firm. Take away from the freezer and place in the fridge for 40 minutes before serving to soften. It should be semisoft.
- You can frozen up the pie up to 3 days. Use plastic wrap to cover after 4 hours then use heavy-duty foil to wrap.
- You can also make the pie in a 9-in. or 24-cm springform pan. Press the crumb mixture onto its bottom and 1 in. up the sides.

Nutrition Information

- Calories: 491

- Total Carbohydrate: 49 g
- Cholesterol: 97 mg
- Total Fat: 30 g
- Fiber: 2 g
- Protein: 6 g
- Sodium: 142 mg
- Saturated Fat: 18 g

59. Gerry's Margarita

"There's nothing like a margarita that is made with the perfect balance of fresh ingredients. One fool-proof tip is to use two tablespoonfuls of white sugar and let the mixture rest after shaking it, most of the sugar will remain in the shaker. The water from ice balances the taste."
Serving: 1 | Prep: 10m | Ready in: 10m

Ingredients

- 1 lime, juiced
- 1/2 lemon, juiced
- 2 tbsps. white sugar
- 2 (1.5 fluid oz.) jiggers reposado tequila (such as Jose Cuervo® Gold)
- 1 cup ice cubes, or as needed
- salt as needed
- 1 tsp. brandy-based orange liqueur (such as Grand Marnier®), or to taste (optional)

Direction

- Press lemon juice and lime juice into a cocktail shaker and add sugar on top. Add in tequila on top of the sugar mixture then put in ice. Cover and shake. Set the shaker aside for 1-2 minutes.
- Place salt in a plate. Run a lemon on the rim of the margarita glass then press the rim in the plate of salt to coat. Transfer margarita in the margarita glass then pour in brandy-based orange liqueur on top.

Nutrition Information

- Calories: 322 calories;
- Total Carbohydrate: 32.2 g
- Cholesterol: 0 mg

- Total Fat: 0 g
- Protein: 0.2 g
- Sodium: 164 mg

60. Gingerade Cadillac

"This recipe adds a new impressive twist on a Cadillac Margarita. A refreshing and delicious drink. Add a lime wedge to garnish if desired."
Serving: 1 | Prep: 5m | Ready in: 5m

Ingredients

- 4 fluid oz. gingerade
- 2 fluid oz. anejo (aged) tequila
- 1 tbsp. fresh lime juice
- ice cubes

Direction

- In a cocktail shaker, combine lime juice, tequila and gingerade. Pour over ice and serve.

Nutrition Information

- Calories: 182 calories;
- Total Carbohydrate: 13.5 g
- Cholesterol: 0 mg
- Total Fat: 0.1 g
- Protein: 0.1 g
- Sodium: 6 mg

61. Gourmet Gelly Shots: Orange Margarita!

"Margaritas can be enjoyed even without using a glass."
Serving: 12 | Prep: 10m | Ready in: 8h10m

Ingredients

- 1 cup boiling water
- 1 (6 oz.) package cherry Jell-O®
- 1/2 cup tequila
- 1/4 cup triple sec

- 1/4 cup orange liqueur (such as Grand Marnier®)

Direction

- In a baking sheet, place twelve 2oz plastic cups.
- While mixing, gradually pour boiling water on a bowl with gelatin mix. Keep on whisking while pouring in orange liqueur, triple sec, and tequila. Transfer mixture in plastic cups.
- Place in the refrigerator for 8 hours to overnight until set.

Nutrition Information

- Calories: 109 calories;
- Total Carbohydrate: 16.6 g
- Cholesterol: 0 mg
- Total Fat: 0 g
- Protein: 1.3 g
- Sodium: 65 mg

62. Grand Margarita

"My husband loves to serve this cocktail drink on every special occasion. No sugar needed in this recipe!"
Serving: 6 | Prep: 10m | Ready in: 10m

Ingredients

- 3 cups water
- 1 1/2 cups fresh lime juice
- 1 1/2 cups cointreau
- 1 1/2 cups silver tequila
- 1 lime, cut into 8 wedges
- coarse salt

Direction

- In a half-gallon pitcher, mix and stir tequila, Cointreau, water, and lime juice thoroughly.
- To serve, rub the rim of a margarita glass using lime and dip into the salt. Pour the tequila mixture into the glass filled with ice. Style the glass with a slice of lime.

63. Grapefruit Margaritas

""What a refreshing margarita with lime and grapefruit!"
Serving: 4 | Prep: 5m | Ready in: 5m

Ingredients

- 1 (12 fluid oz.) can frozen limeade
- 1 1/2 cups tequila
- 1 1/2 cups ruby red grapefruit juice
- 1 1/2 cups ice
- 4 lime wedges, for garnish

Direction

- In a blender, mix grapefruit juice, the limeade, ice, and tequila to blend until smooth. Garnish with lime wedges, serve in glasses.

64. Grateful Dead

"This cocktail includes cola, raspberry liqueur, triple sec, tequila, rum and vodka."
Serving: 1 | Prep: 5m | Ready in: 5m

Ingredients

- 1/4 fluid oz. vodka
- 1/4 fluid oz. rum
- 1/4 fluid oz. tequila
- 1/4 fluid oz. triple sec liqueur
- 1/4 fluid oz. raspberry flavored liqueur
- 2 fluid oz. cola-flavored carbonated beverage

Direction

- Combine raspberry liqueur, triple sec, tequila, rum and vodka over ice in a rock glass. Add cola to taste on top.

65. Grateful Dead Cocktail

"They said that this drink is the sweeter cousin of Long Island ice tea. Try it so that you'll believe it!"
Serving: 1 | Prep: 5m | Ready in: 5m

Ingredients

- 1 fluid oz. tequila
- 1 fluid oz. vodka
- 1 fluid oz. light rum
- 1 fluid oz. gin
- 1 fluid oz. raspberry-flavored liqueur (such as Chambord®)
- 1 cup ice
- 1 tbsp. sour mix

Direction

- Mix gin, rum, tequila, raspberry liqueur, and vodka in a highball glass. Add some ice and top it with a sour mix. Serve.

Nutrition Information

- Calories: 403 calories;
- Total Carbohydrate: 19.3 g
- Cholesterol: 0 mg
- Total Fat: 0.1 g
- Protein: 0 g
- Sodium: 11 mg

66. Grilled Grapefruit Paloma Cocktail

"The traditional Mexican cocktail is fired up with a twist. Caramelize the fruit by grilling lime and grapefruit to give a subtle smoky edges to the juice. Stir in mescal or tequila and pour club soda over the top. You'll have a perfect and refreshing summer drink."
Serving: 2 | Prep: 20m | Ready in: 25m

Ingredients

- 2 limes
- 1/4 cup white sugar
- 1 red grapefruit, halved widthwise
- 1/4 cup kosher salt
- 1 cup ice cubes, or as needed
- 4 fluid oz. tequila
- 2 tbsps. simple syrup, or to taste
- 4 fluid oz. club soda

Direction

- Preheat to medium-high an outdoor grill and oil the grate lightly.
- Halve the limes widthwise. Cut 1 lime half to get 3 wheels.
- In a shallow bowl, add the sugar. Dip grapefruit, 2 lime wheels and the lime halves into it till thoroughly coated.
- On the hot grill, place grapefruit and limes with the cut side facing down. Cook for 5-10 minutes, occasionally turn the lime wheels till browned and it forms grill marks. Place on a rimmed baking sheet and let cool.
- Use the leftover lime wheel to rub over the rim of 2 highball glasses. Coat the rims with kosher salt by dipping them in. Add ice to fill the glasses.
- In a small pitcher, juice grapefruit and grilled lime halves. If there's any juices accumulated on the baking sheet, pour in then stir in simple syrup and tequila. Transfer into glasses and pour club soda over the top. Add grilled lime wheels for garnish.

Nutrition Information

- Calories: 344 calories;
- Total Carbohydrate: 56.4 g
- Cholesterol: 0 mg
- Total Fat: 0.1 g
- Protein: 1.5 g
- Sodium: 11394 mg

"The Paloma is Mexico's most popular cocktail. This recipe is the farcified version with a slightly smoky edge from the grilled lime and grilled fresh grapefruit."
Serving: Makes 2 drinks

Ingredients

- 1 medium to large yellow or pink grapefruit, halved
- 2 limes, halved
- Kosher salt or coarse sea salt, for the glass
- Ice
- 4 oz. (1/2 cup) tequila
- 1 oz. agave nectar or simple syrup (see Note)
- 2 oz. club soda

Direction

- Preheat a grill pan or light and set a grill directly on heat. Over high heat, grill the limes and grapefruit for 4-5 minutes till the bottom is well browned. Allow to cool slightly.
- Pour some salt on a small plate. Moisten then coat the rims of 2 highball glasses with salt.
- To make each cocktail: Add ice to fill a shaker then place in 1/2 oz. agave nectar, 2 oz. of tequila, 1 oz. of squeezed lime juice and 2 oz. of squeezed grapefruit juice. Cover then shake well. Add ice to fill one of the prepped glasses and strain in the drink. Add 1 oz. of club soda on top and serve. Add clean ice to fill the shaker to make another cocktail.
- To prepare simple syrup: Combine 1/2 cup of water and 1/2 cup of sugar in a saucepan over medium high heat then stir till the sugar dissolves. Allow to cool slightly. For this recipe, measure and use 1/2 cup then save up the rest for use later.

"A quick sizzle on the grill can transform an ordinary lb. cake into an extraordinary and singular dessert. Especially you pair it with tequila-scented whipped cream and a pineapple salsa."
Serving: Makes 4 servings

Ingredients

- 3/4 cup heavy (whipping) cream
- 3 tbsps. confectioners' sugar
- 1/4 tsp. ground cinnamon
- 1 tbsp. tequila (preferably gold)
- 8 slices lb. cake (each 1/2 inch thick)
- 2 to 3 tbsps. unsalted butter, melted
- Pineapple "Salsa"
- 4 fresh mint sprigs, for garnish

Direction

- In a large metal bowl or a chilled mixer bowl, place the cream and use a mixer to beat for 6-8 minutes in total till it forms soft peaks. Start beating on the low speed then slowly increase to high speed. Once it has formed soft peaks, add tequila, cinnamon and confectioners' sugar. Keep beating for 2 more minutes till it forms stiff peaks. To prevent the cream turning into butter, don't overbeat it. You can make the tequila whipped cream several hours ahead then cover and store in the fridge till ready to serve.
- Lightly brush butter on both sides of each lb. cake slice. Follow the instructions below for any of the grills to cook the lb. cake till toasted lightly. If you want to leave a handsome crosshatch of grill the marks, after 1 minute, give each slice a quarter turn. The lb. cake slices may need to be cooked in more than 1 batch.
- On a plate, place the lb. cake slices with a dollop of tequila whipped cream and a spoonful of Pineapple "Salsa" on top. Add a

sprig of mint to garnish then serve immediately.

- For contact grill: Preheat the grill; set to high if there's a temperature control on your grill. Place under the grill's front with a drip pan. Lightly apply oil on the surface of the grill once ready to cook. On the hot grill, place lb. cake slices and close the lid. Cook the lb. cake for 2-4 minutes till done.
- For grill pan: Preheat the grill pan on the stove over medium heat till medium-high. A drop of water will skitter in the grill pan when it gets hot. Once ready to cook, lightly apply oil on the grill pan's ridges. In the hot grill pan, place the lb. cake slices. Cook the lb. cake for 2-4 minutes each side till done.
- Built-in grill: Preheat the grill to high then, if the surface isn't nonstick, brush and apply oil on the grill grate. On the hot grate, place the slices of lb. cake. Cook for 2-4 minutes each side till done.
- Freestanding grill: Preheat the grill to high. You don't need to oil the grate. On the hot grill, place the slices of lb. cake. Cook for 3-5 minutes per side till done.
- Fireplace grill: Under the gridiron, rake the red hot embers then preheat it for 3-5 minutes. You want a hot, 2 to 3 Mississippi fire. Brush and apply oil on the gridiron once ready to cook. On the hot grate, place the slices of lb. cake. Cook for 2-4 minutes each side till done.
- You can use any kind of indoor grill to toast the lb. cake. The grill pan will gives you tack-sharp grill marks.

69. Hilton Head Iced Tea

"This recipe is similar to Long Island iced tea but it was added a mule kick. A great drink for humid and hot days."
Serving: 2 | Prep: 10m | Ready in: 10m

Ingredients

- ice, as needed
- 4 fluid oz. beer (such as Miller® High Life®)
- 3 fluid oz. orange juice
- 1/2 fluid oz. vodka
- 1/2 fluid oz. gin
- 1/2 fluid oz. white rum
- 1/2 fluid oz. silver tequila
- 1/2 fluid oz. triple sec
- 3 fluid oz. cola-flavored carbonated beverage (such as Coca-Cola®), or more as needed

Direction

- Add ice to fill a pitcher. Gently stir in triple sec, tequila, rum, gin, vodka, orange juice and beer. Add ice to fill tall glasses. Fill each glass with the drink mixture. Add cola-flavored beverage to top off each drink.

Nutrition Information

- Calories: 159 calories;
- Total Carbohydrate: 15.1 g
- Cholesterol: 0 mg
- Total Fat: 0.1 g
- Protein: 0.6 g
- Sodium: 20 mg

70. Horchata Margarita

"My friends would always look for this drink whenever I hosted a party at my house. You'll love it!"
Serving: 1 | Prep: 5m | Ready in: 5m

Ingredients

- ice
- 8 tbsps. horchata
- 1 1/2 fluid oz. silver tequila
- 1 fluid oz. rum cream liqueur (such as RumChata®)
- 1/4 fluid oz. agave nectar
- 1/4 fluid oz. cinnamon whiskey (such as Fireball®)
- 1 tsp. sweetened condensed milk, or to taste
- 1 dash ground cinnamon

Direction

- Pour ice in a cocktail shaker together with cinnamon whiskey, rum cream liqueur, tequila, horchata, and agave. Shake the shaker until the drink is fully chilled.
- Touch the rim of the margarita glass in a condensed milk. Sprinkle cinnamon. Transfer the horchata mixture into the glass.

Nutrition Information

- Calories: 285 calories;
- Total Carbohydrate: 25.8 g
- Cholesterol: 2 mg
- Total Fat: 6.9 g
- Protein: 2.9 g
- Sodium: 15 mg

71. Island Iced Tea

Serving: Serves 2

Ingredients

- 1 pony (1 oz.) light tequila
- 1 pony (1 oz.) light rum
- 1 pony (1 oz.) gin
- 1 pony (1 oz.) vodka
- 1 oz. (1 pony) Triple Sec
- 1 pony (1 oz.) fresh lemon juice
- 1/3 cup cola
- Garnish: 2 lemon slices

Direction

- Combine lemon juice, Triple Sec, vodka, gin, rum and tequila in a cocktail shaker with half of it filled with ice cubes. Shake for 30 seconds and strain the mixture into 2 ice cubes-filled tall glasses. Pour cola into glasses and add lemon slices to garnish.

72. Italian Amaretto Margaritas

"The fun twist of this drink comes from the amaretto. It's even better when served in frosty glasses rimmed with sugar and amaretto."
Serving: 4 | Prep: 10m | Ready in: 10m

Ingredients

- 4 fluid oz. amaretto liqueur, plus additional
- white sugar
- 6 fluid oz. frozen limeade concentrate
- 6 fluid oz. tequila
- 1/2 cup orange juice
- 6 cups ice

Direction

- Get 4 margarita glasses and dip their rims respectively into amaretto and sugar; put aside. In the blender's bowl, add ice, orange juice, amaretto, tequila and lime aid. Puree till smooth then transfer to prepped glasses.

73. Italian Amaretto Margaritas On The Rocks

"A different variation of Italian Margaritas."
Serving: 4 | Prep: 5m | Ready in: 5m

Ingredients

- 2 tbsps. confectioners' sugar
- 4 cups crushed ice
- 2 cups sweet and sour mix
- 5 fluid oz. tequila
- 5 fluid oz. amaretto (almond-flavored liqueur)
- 2 fluid oz. orange liqueur
- 4 orange slices for garnish
- 4 lime slices for garnish

Direction

- Dampen slightly the rims of four 12oz glasses then press in confectioners' sugar to the rim of the glasses. Put each with crushed ice.

- In a pitcher, mix orange liqueur, sweet and sour mix, amaretto, and tequila together. Stir. Transfer mixture in the prepared glasses. Add lime and orange slices on each glass to garnish.

74. Jalapeno And Cucumber Margarita

"The freshness from cucumber will make each bite of tequila and jalapeno tasty ever."
Serving: 4 | Prep: 5m | Ready in: 1h5m

Ingredients

- 1/2 cup tequila, or more to taste
- 1/2 cup fresh lime juice
- 1/4 cup orange liqueur
- 1/4 cup simple syrup
- 1 jalapeno pepper, halved and seeded
- 4 thin slices cucumber, or more to taste
- 4 wedges lime
- 2 tbsps. kosher salt, or as needed
- ice, as needed
- 4 slices cucumber

Direction

- In a pitcher with a lid, stir tequila, simple syrup, lime juice, and orange liqueur together. Add in thin cucumber slices and jalapeno pepper. Refrigerate for at least 60 minutes.
- Take a wedge of lime to run along the rim of each of four pint glasses. Drizzle kosher salt on a flat plate; coat by pressing glass rims into salt. Add ice into glass and pour in margarita. Garnish cucumber slice.

Nutrition Information

- Calories: 170 calories;
- Total Carbohydrate: 20.7 g
- Cholesterol: 0 mg
- Total Fat: 0.1 g
- Protein: 0.5 g
- Sodium: 2887 mg

75. Jalapeno Margaritas

"The agave nectar and fresh lime juice will surprise you"
Serving: 2 | Prep: 10m | Ready in: 10m

Ingredients

- kosher salt
- ice cubes
- 4 fluid oz. tequila
- 2 fluid oz. triple sec
- 2 limes, juiced
- 1 tbsp. agave nectar
- 1/2 jalapeno pepper, seeded and diced
- 1 limes, cut into wedges

Direction

- On a small, shallow plate, pour 1/4 to 1/2 inch of salt. Use water to moisten the rim of two margarita glasses and dip into the salt. Fill with ice, and take aside.
- In a cocktail shaker, pour the tequila, agave nectar, jalapeno, triple sec, and lime juice over ice. Take a cover, shaking vigorously until the outside of the shaker is frozen. Pour into the prepared glasses, and garnish lime wedges and serve.

Nutrition Information

- Calories: 298 calories;
- Total Carbohydrate: 32.1 g
- Cholesterol: 0 mg
- Total Fat: 0.3 g
- Protein: 0.8 g
- Sodium: 212 mg

76. Jewel's Watermelon Margaritas

"This non-frozen version of watermelon margarita is so astounding and reviving on sweltering summer days. You can use lemon-lime soda instead of tequila if you want to make a virgin version of this."
Serving: 4 | Prep: 10m | Ready in: 45m

Ingredients

- 1/2 cup white sugar
- 1/2 cup water
- 3 strips orange zest
- 2 cups cubed seeded watermelon
- 3/4 cup white tequila
- 1/4 cup lime juice
- salt or sugar for rimming glasses (optional)
- 1 lime, cut into wedges
- 2 cups crushed ice, or as needed

Direction

- Boil 1/2cup of sugar, orange zest, and water in a small saucepan, stirring the mixture constantly. Bring it to simmer for 3 minutes until the sugar has dissolved. Remove the simple syrup from the heat and let it cool completely.
- Blend watermelon in a blender or food processor and pulse until pureed.
- Pour the watermelon puree into a large pitcher together with the simple syrup, lime juice, and tequila.
- Drop a small amount of salt or sugar in a saucer. Rub lime wedge into the rim of margarita glasses to moisten. Lightly dip the rim of the glass into the saucer to rim the glass. Tap off excess salt or sugar.
- Pour crushed ice into the rimmed glasses. Distribute the margarita mixture among the glasses and garnish them with lime wedges before serving.

Nutrition Information

- Calories: 241 calories;
- Total Carbohydrate: 37.5 g
- Cholesterol: 0 mg
- Total Fat: 0.2 g
- Protein: 0.9 g
- Sodium: 44 mg

77. Joe's Perfect 'anti~sour Mix' Margarita

""This margarita is a must-try! It's more unique than any other margarita recipe that has a stomach-upsetting sour mix.""
Serving: 1 | Prep: 10m | Ready in: 10m

Ingredients

- kosher salt
- 1 cup ice cubes
- 2 fluid oz. silver tequila
- 1 fluid oz. orange liqueur
- 1 fluid oz. sweetened lime juice (such as Rose's®)
- 2 oz. grapefruit flavored soda

Direction

- Place 1/4-1/2-inch of salt in a small and shallow plate. Use water to moisten the rim of the large glass. Dip the rim into the salt. Place the ice in a glass and set it aside.
- In a cocktail shaker filled with ice, pour in orange liqueur, lime juice, and tequila. Cover and shake the shaker until it's frosty. Strain the mixture into the prepared glass. Pour in grapefruit soda slowly before serving.

Nutrition Information

- Calories: 314 calories;
- Total Carbohydrate: 30.3 g
- Cholesterol: 0 mg
- Total Fat: 0.1 g
- Protein: 0 g
- Sodium: 411 mg

78. Keto Margarita

"You won't feel any guilt drinking this keto margarita. To imitate the taste of the orange liqueur, I added the orange-flavored sparkling water and I also use Swerve® instead of sugar."
Serving: 1 | Prep: 10m | Ready in: 10m

Ingredients

- 3 cups ice
- 2 fluid oz. tequila
- 1 fluid oz. lime juice
- 2 1/2 tsps. low-calorie natural sweetener (such as Swerve®)
- 1 tbsp. coarse salt
- 2 lime wedges
- 1 pint-sized Mason jar
- 2 fluid oz. orange-flavored sparkling water (such as La Croix®)

Direction

- Place ice in a shaker to half-full. Add the sweetener, lime juice, and tequila. Cover the shaker and shake thoroughly for 10-15 seconds until the outside is frosty.
- Put the salt on a plate. Use a lime wedge to run the rim of the Mason jar. Dip the jar down into the salt. Place the ice cubes in a jar.
- Strain the margarita drink into the jar and top it with sparkling water; stir. Garnish the drink with the remaining lime wedge.

Nutrition Information

- Calories: 142 calories;
- Total Carbohydrate: 3.6 g
- Cholesterol: 0 mg
- Total Fat: 0 g
- Protein: 0.2 g
- Sodium: 5785 mg

79. Kim's Peach Margarita

"This delicious peach margarita is a perfect adult summer drink. You can adjust the amounts of every ingredient depending on your preference."
Serving: 2 | Prep: 10m | Ready in: 10m

Ingredients

- 1 cup fresh peaches - peeled, pitted and sliced
- 3/4 cup peach nectar
- 1 cup ice
- 2 fluid oz. tequila
- 2 fluid oz. triple sec

Direction

- In a blender, blend triple sec, peaches, tequila, peach nectar and ice together until mixture becomes smooth.

Nutrition Information

- Calories: 238 calories;
- Total Carbohydrate: 30.2 g
- Cholesterol: 0 mg
- Total Fat: 0.1 g
- Protein: 0.3 g
- Sodium: 15 mg

80. Kiwi Margarita

"Make a zippy twist on the classic margaritas with kiwis."
Serving: 4 | Prep: 5m | Ready in: 5m

Ingredients

- 1/2 cup superfine sugar
- 1/3 cup gold tequila
- 1/3 cup triple sec
- 2 large kiwis, peeled
- 1 cup fresh lime juice
- 2 cups small ice cubes

Direction

- In a blender filled with ice cubes, blend lime juice, tequila, sugar, kiwis and triple sec together until smooth.

---

81. La Vida Mezcal

"This drink is added with a delicious smoky quality with just a touch of mezcal. Make sure to use the good quality tequila and mescal. You can use Aperol instead of Campari and adjust the ratios of sweet vermouth-Campari and tequila-mezcal."
Serving: 1 | Prep: 3m | Ready in: 3m

Ingredients

- ice
- 1 1/2 fluid oz. tequila
- 1/2 fluid oz. mezcal
- 3/4 fluid oz. sweet vermouth
- 3/4 fluid oz. bitter orange aperitif (such as Campari® or Aperol®)
- 1 dash orange bitters
- 1 thin slice orange

Direction

- In a cocktail shaker, place ice and add Campari, vermouth, mezcal and tequila. Place in a dash of bitters then shake or stir. In a rock glass filled with ice, strain the drink and add a slice of orange to garnish.

Nutrition Information

- Calories: 168 calories;
- Total Carbohydrate: 3.7 g
- Cholesterol: 0 mg
- Total Fat: 0 g
- Protein: 0.1 g
- Sodium: 10 mg

---

82. Larbo's Mango Margarita

"A refreshing and delicious mango margarita. Top off the margarita with a thin layer Grand Marnier to get an extra special twist."
Serving: 2 | Prep: 10m | Ready in: 10m

Ingredients

- 4 fluid oz. tequila
- 1 fluid oz. triple sec liqueur
- 1 mango, peeled and seeded
- 2 fluid oz. water
- 2 cups crushed ice

Direction

- Combine ice, water, mango, triple sec and tequila in a blender. Process till smooth.

---

83. Lauren's Grapefruit Margaritas

"Lime and grapefruit are a great combo for a lovely margarita! Fresh juice is so much better but in case you don't have much time to make one, store-bought ones also taste good."
Serving: 4 | Prep: 10m | Ready in: 10m

Ingredients

- 1 cup fresh grapefruit juice
- 1 cup fresh lime juice
- 1/2 cup triple sec
- 1/2 cup tequila
- 1 tbsp. agave syrup
- 1 cup ice cubes
- 1 tbsp. pomegranate seeds (optional)

Direction

- In a pitcher, combine the triple sec, grapefruit juice, agave syrup, lime juice and tequila together add in the ice cubes and then mix. Strain the cocktail mixture directly into 4 margarita glasses then put a couple pomegranate seeds into each glass and serve.

- Calories: 235 calories;
- Total Carbohydrate: 29.4 g
- Cholesterol: 0 mg
- Total Fat: 0.2 g
- Protein: 0.6 g
- Sodium: 6 mg

84. Layered Margarita Jell-o® Shots

"A traditional and colorful cocktail."
Serving: 12 | Prep: 10m | Ready in: 12h10m

Ingredients

- 2 1/2 cups boiling water, divided
- 1 (3 oz.) package lime-flavored gelatin mix (such as Jell-O®), divided
- 1 cup tequila, divided
- 2 (0.3 oz.) packages sugar-free orange gelatin mix (such as Jell-O®)
- 1/4 cup triple sec

Direction

- In a glass measuring cup, place 1/2 of the lime-flavored gelatin then stir in a cup of boiling water until the gelatin dissolves; mix in half cup tequila. Pour mixture in 12 two-oz. cups until 1/3 full.
- Place in the refrigerator for 4 hours until set.
- In a glass measuring cup, mix orange gelatin mixes and half cup boiling water together until the gelatin dissolves. Mix in Triple Sec. Take the cups out of the refrigerator. In each cup, layer the orange gelatin mixture until half as tall as the lime mixture.
- Place in the refrigerator for 4 hours until set.
- In a glass measuring cup, mix the remaining lime-flavored gelatin and a cup of boiling water together until the gelatin dissolves; mix in the remaining half cup tequila. Take the cups out of the refrigerator. Layer lime-tequila mixture over the cup as tall as the bottom layer.
- Place in the refrigerator for 4 hours until set.

Nutrition Information

- Calories: 88 calories;
- Total Carbohydrate: 8.4 g
- Cholesterol: 0 mg
- Total Fat: 0 g
- Protein: 0.7 g
- Sodium: 34 mg

85. Lemon Margarita

Serving: Makes 4 drinks

Ingredients

- 1/3 cup fresh lemon juice
- 1 cup white Tequila
- 1/3 cup Triple Sec
- Coarse salt for coating the rims of the glasses

Direction

- In lemon juice, dunk the rims of four long-stemmed glasses then place in the freezer. Mix about two cups of crushed ice, Tequila, remaining lemon juice, and Triple sec together in a sealable pitcher or bottle; secure lid and shake well until really cold and the ice nearly melts. Take the glasses out of the freezer and press the rims in salt. Shake off the extra salt then put in ice cubes until full. Split Margaritas between the glasses.

Nutrition Information

- Calories: 204
- Total Carbohydrate: 9 g
- Total Fat: 0 g
- Fiber: 0 g
- Protein: 0 g
- Sodium: 231 mg
- Saturated Fat: 0 g

86. Limeshot Mexi-martini

"This margarita martini recipe isn't too sweet and there's a surprise of a yummy tequila-lime gelatin shot at the glass's bottom."
Serving: 4 | Prep: 15m | Ready in: 1h15m

Ingredients

- 1 (3 oz.) package lime-flavored gelatin mix (such as Jell-O®)
- 1 cup boiling water
- 1 cup tequila
- coarse salt, as needed
- 1 cup ice cubes, or as needed
- 1 cup margarita mix
- 1/2 cup tequila
- 1 (12 fluid oz.) can or bottle beer
- 1 lime, sliced

Direction

- In a bowl, combine boiling water and lime-flavored gelatin mix. Stir till gelatin melts. Add into gelatin mixture 1 cup of tequila and stir. Add in about 24 shot glasses and refrigerate at least 1 hour to set.
- Salt 4-6 martini glasses' rims.
- In a cocktail shaker, mix 1/2 cup of tequila, margarita mix and ice in; shake till well mixed. In each prepped martini glass's bottom, place a lime-flavored gelatin shot. Pour over the shot with margarita mixture but leave space enough to top with beer. Use beer to top each margarita-martini and uses lime slice to garnish.

Nutrition Information

- Calories: 371 calories;
- Total Carbohydrate: 36.2 g
- Cholesterol: 0 mg
- Total Fat: 0 g
- Protein: 2.2 g
- Sodium: 102 mg

87. Long Island Iced Tea

"It's a strong drink, but with a very delicate taste. You won't realize that you're drinking some alcohol. Mix them up with top shelf liquors. Have fun!"
Serving: 1 | Prep: 5m | Ready in: 5m

Ingredients

- 1 (1.5 fluid oz.) jigger vodka
- 1 (1.5 fluid oz.) jigger gin
- 1 (1.5 fluid oz.) jigger rum
- 1 (1.5 fluid oz.) jigger triple sec liqueur
- 1 tsp. tequila
- 2 tsps. orange juice
- 2 fluid oz. cola-flavored carbonated beverage
- 1 wedge lemon

Direction

- Fill the cocktail mixer with full ice and stir in gin, triple sec, tequila, rum, and vodka. Mix in cola and orange juice. Shake the mixer vigorously until foamy. Transfer the mixture into the Collins glass and fill it with ice. Garnish the glass with lemon wedge before serving.

Nutrition Information

- Calories: 507 calories;
- Total Carbohydrate: 28.9 g
- Cholesterol: 0 mg
- Total Fat: 0.2 g
- Protein: 0.3 g
- Sodium: 8 mg

88. Long Island Iced Tea Cocktail

"This intense blend of five different liquors was improved by cola and simple syrup for a hazardously delectable drink."
Serving: 1 | Prep: 5m | Ready in: 5m

Ingredients

- 3/4 fluid oz. vodka
- 3/4 fluid oz. tequila
- 3/4 fluid oz. gin
- 3/4 fluid oz. light rum
- 3/4 fluid oz. triple sec
- 1/2 fluid oz. simple syrup
- 1/2 fluid oz. lemon juice
- 1/2 cup ice
- 1 fluid oz. cola

Direction

- In a highball glass, mix triple sec, lemon juice, gin, tequila, simple syrup, rum, and vodka. Fill the glass with ice and add color by pouring in cola.

Nutrition Information

- Calories: 332 calories;
- Total Carbohydrate: 23.9 g
- Cholesterol: 0 mg
- Total Fat: 0.1 g
- Protein: 0.1 g
- Sodium: 8 mg

89. Lori's Creamy Strawberry Tequila

""This delicious and creamy drink is a mixture of strawberry flavor and tequila. My mother-in-law gave me this recipe, and I love it!""
Serving: 8 | Prep: 10m | Ready in: 10m

Ingredients

- 1 (14 oz.) can sweetened condensed milk
- 1 pint half-and-half cream
- 1/2 cup vodka
- 1/2 cup strawberry schnapps
- 1/3 cup tequila
- 3 tbsps. vanilla extract
- 2 tbsps. strawberry syrup
- 1 cup ice, or as needed

Direction

- Fill the blender with ice, half-and-half, tequila, syrup, vanilla extract, sweetened condensed milk, vodka, and schnapps. Blend the mixture until smooth. You can drink it on the rocks or as shots.

90. Magnificent Frozen Mango Margaritas

"This drink is ideal for Cinco de Mayo or any other day of the year! If desired, decorate the glass with kosher salt or coarse sugar."
Serving: 4 | Prep: 10m | Ready in: 10m

Ingredients

- 1 cup ice, or as needed
- 1 cup frozen mango chunks
- 3 fluid oz. tequila
- 3 fluid oz. triple sec
- 3 fluid oz. ginger ale (such as Vernors®)
- 3 fluid oz. simple syrup
- 1 1/2 fluid oz. lemon juice

Direction

- In a blender, blend lemon juice, ice, tequila, mango, triple sec, simple syrup, and ginger ale until smooth.

Nutrition Information

- Calories: 220 calories;
- Total Carbohydrate: 34 g
- Cholesterol: 0 mg
- Total Fat: 0.2 g
- Protein: 0.3 g
- Sodium: 8 mg

91. Mama D's Very Berry Margaritas

""This frozen margarita is best when served on a festive occasion or on a hot day. This refreshing drink is cool, sweet, and smooth.""
Serving: 6 | Prep: 10m | Ready in: 10m

Ingredients

- 3 cups ice
- 1 cup gold tequila
- 2/3 cup triple sec
- 1/2 cup orange juice
- 2/3 cup frozen strawberries
- 2/3 cup frozen blueberries
- 2/3 cup frozen raspberries
- 3 tbsps. white sugar

Direction

- Fill the blender pitcher with ice. Pour in a triple sec, orange juice, and tequila. Add the sugar, raspberries, strawberries, and blueberries. Cover the pitcher and blend the mixture until smooth or until its desired consistency is reached. Pour the mixture into the chilled glasses. Serve.

Nutrition Information

- Calories: 245 calories;
- Total Carbohydrate: 26.6 g
- Cholesterol: 0 mg
- Total Fat: 0.3 g
- Protein: 0.5 g
- Sodium: 7 mg

92. Mandarin Margaritas

"It's a perfect combination of tequila and fresh juice. As you see, the tequila makes my spirit alive, while the fresh juice makes me feel like I'm healthy. Agave honey is a perfect alternative for sugar, it makes the margarita tastes more delicate."
Serving: 2 | Prep: 5m | Ready in: 5m

Ingredients

- 1 cup fresh tangerine juice
- 1 cup ice
- 2 (1.5 fluid oz.) jiggers premium tequila blanco
- 1 tbsp. agave nectar

Direction

- Mix tequila, agave nectar, tangerine juice, and ice in a blender. Blend the mixture until the ice is crushed completely. Pour it into 2 margarita glasses. Serve.

Nutrition Information

- Calories: 180 calories;
- Total Carbohydrate: 20.5 g
- Cholesterol: 0 mg
- Total Fat: 0.2 g
- Protein: 0.6 g
- Sodium: 5 mg

93. Mango Frozen Margarita

Serving: Serves 2

Ingredients

- 1 1/2 cups diced peeled ripe mango
- 3 oz (about 1/3 cup) white tequila
- 1 oz (2 tbsps.) Cointreau or other orange liqueur
- 2 oz (1/4 cup) fresh lime juice
- 3 tbsps. superfine granulated sugar
- 2 cups ice cubes

Direction

- In a blender, blend all the ingredients till smooth.

Nutrition Information

- Calories: 296
- Total Carbohydrate: 44 g
- Total Fat: 1 g
- Fiber: 2 g
- Protein: 1 g
- Sodium: 13 mg
- Saturated Fat: 0 g

---

94. Mangorita

"The border Mango Margaritas with its authentic south."
Serving: 1 | Prep: 5m | Ready in: 5m

Ingredients

- 2 (1.5 fluid oz.) jiggers tequila
- 1 (1.5 fluid oz.) jigger triple sec liqueur
- 1 (1.5 fluid oz.) jigger fresh lime juice
- 1 mango - peeled, seeded, and sliced
- 4 ice cubes
- 1/4 cup mango nectar

Direction

- Combine ice, mango, lime juice, triple sec and tequila in a blender. Blend to finely crush the ice. Add mango nectar to sweeten to your taste.

---

95. Manly Margarita

"One of my favorite margarita without blender, salt, or silly glass."
Serving: 1 | Prep: 10m | Ready in: 10m

Ingredients

- 1/2 cup ice cubes, or as desired
- 2 (1.5 fluid oz.) jiggers tequila plata
- 1 (1.5 fluid oz.) jigger triple sec
- 1 (1.5 fluid oz.) jigger lime juice

Direction

- Fill ice; add tequila, lime juice, and triple sec in a rocks glass, stirring. Let margarita rest for 2 minutes.

Nutrition Information

- Calories: 364 calories;
- Total Carbohydrate: 23.5 g
- Cholesterol: 0 mg
- Total Fat: 0.2 g
- Protein: 0.2 g
- Sodium: 8 mg

---

96. Margarita

"This drink tastes even better even without the triple sec."
Serving: Makes 1

Ingredients

- Kosher salt (for serving)
- 1/2-inch thick lime wheel (for serving)
- 2 oz. tequila blanco
- 3/4 oz. fresh lime juice
- 3/4 oz. simple syrup

Direction

- Put salt in a small plate. Run lime (reserve for serving) on the rim of rocks or old-fashioned glass then press in the salt. Fill the glass with ice then set it aside.
- In a cocktail shaker, mix simple syrup, lime juice, and tequila together then fill with ice; cover and shake well for about 20secs until the outside of shaker is very cold.
- With a slotted spoon or Hawthorne strainer, filter cocktail to the prepared glass. Add a lime wheel to garnish.

Nutrition Information

- Calories: 193

- Total Carbohydrate: 17 g
- Total Fat: 0 g
- Fiber: 0 g
- Protein: 0 g
- Sodium: 13 mg
- Saturated Fat: 0 g

97. Margarita Cheesecake

*"This irresistible cheesecake is made with light sour cream
and reduced-fat cream cheese."*
Serving: Serves 10 to 12

Ingredients

- Nonstick vegetable oil spray
- 1 1/4 cups graham cracker crumbs
- 1/4 cup (1/2 stick) unsalted butter, melted
- 3 8-oz.
- 1 1/4 cups light sour cream
- 3/4 cup plus 2 tbsps. sugar
- 2 1/2 tbsps. triple sec or other orange liqueur
- 2 1/2 tbsps. tequila
- 2 1/2 tbsps. fresh lime juice
- 4 large eggs
- 3/4 cup light sour cream
- 1 tbsp. fresh lime juice
- 1 tbsp. sugar
- Very thin lime slices, cut in half
- Very thin lime peel strips

Direction

- To make crust: Preheat the oven to 350°F with the rack on the center. Use vegetable oil spray to coat a 9-in. springform pan which has two 3/4-in.-high sides. In a medium bowl, mix butter and graham cracker crumbs till blended. On the prepped pan, press the crumbs on the bottom and 1-in. up on the sides. Store the crust in the fridge.
- To make filling: In a large bowl, beat cheese with an electric mixer till fluffy. Add in and beat sour cream then lime juice, tequila, triple sec and sugar. Add in eggs and beat.
- Spread the filling onto the crust. Bake for 50 minutes till the middle slightly moves when you shake the pan and 2 inches on the outside are set. Take away from the oven and turn it off.
- To make topping: In a small bowl, whisk sugar, lime juice and sour cream till blended. Evenly pour over the cheesecake. Bring the cheesecake back to the hot oven. Allow to stand for no more than 45 minutes. The cheesecake should look soft but when chilled, it'll set up. Store the cake for up to 1 day in the fridge till well chilled.
- Use a knife to run around the sides and discard the sides of the pan. Transfer onto a platter. Place lime peel and half-slices around the cheesecake's top edge.

Nutrition Information

- Calories: 287
- Total Carbohydrate: 33 g
- Cholesterol: 103 mg
- Total Fat: 14 g
- Fiber: 1 g
- Protein: 5 g
- Sodium: 116 mg
- Saturated Fat: 7 g

98. Margarita Cocktail

*"Any day is a decent day for a margarita. This drink will
give you refreshment on a hot day and will warm you up
on a cold day. It's one of the popular and best drinks I ever
had."*
Serving: 1 | Prep: 5m | Ready in: 5m

Ingredients

- 1 tbsp. kosher salt
- 1 1/2 fluid oz. tequila
- 1 fluid oz. orange flavored liqueur (such as Cointreau®)
- 1/2 fluid oz. lime juice
- 1 cup ice
- 1 lime wheel

Direction

- Put some salt in a small plate. Using a damp paper towel, lightly wet the rim of the margarita glass or cocktail glass. Dip the wet rim part into the salt to coat; put aside.
- In a cocktail shaker, mix lime juice, tequila, and orange-flavored brandy. Fill the shaker with some ice and shake it until frosty. Strain the mixture into the salt rimmed ice filled margarita glass or salt-rimmed cocktail glass.
- Before serving, garnish the glass with a lime wheel.

Nutrition Information

- Calories: 202 calories;
- Total Carbohydrate: 14.1 g
- Cholesterol: 0 mg
- Total Fat: 0.1 g
- Protein: 0.1 g
- Sodium: 5770 mg

99. Margarita Con Cerveza

"This a new twist to a classic which will make everyone crave for more! Feel free to increase the ingredients to serve more people."
Serving: 8 | Prep: 10m | Ready in: 10m

Ingredients

- 1 (12 fluid oz.) can frozen limeade concentrate
- 1 (12 fluid oz.) can or bottle Mexican beer (such as Corona®)
- 1 (12 fluid oz.) can or bottle lemon-lime soda (such as 7-Up®)
- 1 cup tequila
- 1/2 cup triple sec
- 1 lime, halved

Direction

- Into a pitcher, add limeade concentrate and then mix to break into big chunks. Add triple sec, beer, tequila, and lemon-lime soda. Mix thoroughly. Press 1/2 lime into the margarita.

Chop the remaining lime half into wedges and use them to decorate margarita glasses.

Nutrition Information

- Calories: 297 calories;
- Total Carbohydrate: 48.3 g
- Cholesterol: 0 mg
- Total Fat: 0.1 g
- Protein: 0.3 g
- Sodium: 8 mg

100. Margarita I

Serving: Serves 1.

Ingredients

- Cut lime
- Salt
- 2 oz. tequila
- 1/2 oz. Cointreau or Triple Sec
- 1 tbsp. lime juice
- 3 or 4 ice cubes

Direction

- Use lime to rub the rim of a cocktail glass. Dip it into the salt to frost. In a mixing glass, mix the remaining ingredients thoroughly. Strain the drink into the prepared cocktail glass.

101. Margarita Ice Pops

"For a dessert Mexican cocktail, put lightened-up homemade margarita mix in pop molds."
Serving: 8 | Prep: 15m | Ready in: 8h15m

Ingredients

- 1¼ cups plain seltzer
- ¾ cup lime juice
- ⅓ cup white sugar
- ¼ cup tequila
- 2 tbsps. Triple Sec
- Pinch of salt

Direction

- Mix salt, Triple Sec, tequila, sugar, lime juice and seltzer in big measuring cup. Put into 8 2-oz. freezer pop molds. Freeze for at least 8 hours till firm.

Nutrition Information

- Calories: 66 calories;
- Total Carbohydrate: 12 g
- Cholesterol: 0 mg
- Total Fat: 0 g
- Fiber: 0 g
- Protein: 0 g
- Sodium: 19 mg
- Sugar: 10 g
- Saturated Fat: 0 g

102. Margarita Jell-o® Shots

"A yummy margarita-flavored Jell-O® shot recipe! There's a little bit of kick to it so if you want it to be a lot more pleasing to the taste, just replace a bit of the alcohol with water."
Serving: 15 | Prep: 5m | Ready in: 5h5m

Ingredients

- 1 cup boiling water
- 1 (3 oz.) package lime-flavored gelatin mix (such as Jell-O®)
- 1/3 cup tequila
- 1/3 cup triple sec
- 1/3 cup water
- 15 plastic shot glasses, or as needed

Direction

- In a bowl, mix the gelatin mix and boiling water together. Mix well until the gelatin has fully dissolved. Put in the triple sec, water and tequila. Give it another mix.
- Distribute the mixture evenly into the shot glasses. Keep it in the fridge for about 5 hours until the gelatin has set.

Nutrition Information

- Calories: 52 calories;
- Total Carbohydrate: 7.3 g
- Cholesterol: 0 mg
- Total Fat: 0 g
- Protein: 0.5 g
- Sodium: 27 mg

103. Margarita Made Easy

"It's a recipe of the quirkiest yet fastest frozen margarita with a hard-to-beat flavor."
Serving: 4 | Prep: 2m | Ready in: 2m

Ingredients

- 1 (6 oz.) can frozen limeade concentrate
- 4 (1.5 fluid oz.) jiggers tequila
- 6 fluid oz. caffeinated citrus-flavored soda

Direction

- Combine tequila, citrus soda, and limeade concentrate in a blender filled with ice. Blend the mixture until smooth. Pour it into the glasses; serve.

104. Margarita On The Rocks

"The secret to this incredibly delicious margarita is the lemon-lime soda! Try and make this lovely margarita at the comfort of your own home!"
Serving: 2 | Prep: 5m | Ready in: 5m

Ingredients

- kosher salt for rimming glasses (optional)
- ice cubes
- 1/2 cup silver tequila
- 1/4 cup sweetened lime juice (such as Rose's®)
- 1/4 cup triple sec
- 1/4 cup lemon-lime soda, or to taste

Direction

- Coat the rims of 2 margarita glasses with salt and put ice in it. Fill a shaker with ice and put in the triple sec, tequila, lemon-lime soda and sweetened lime juice then shake the mixture vigorously while holding the top of the shaker tightly so that the carbonated soda doesn't spew out of the shaker. Transfer the mixture into the prepared margarita glasses then serve.

Nutrition Information

- Calories: 317 calories;
- Total Carbohydrate: 29.5 g
- Cholesterol: 0 mg
- Total Fat: 0.1 g
- Protein: 0 g
- Sodium: 210 mg

105. Margaritas

"This will be the best margarita that you'll ever taste."
Serving: 4 | Prep: 5m | Ready in: 5m

Ingredients

- 1 (6 oz.) can frozen limeade concentrate
- 6 fluid oz. tequila
- 2 fluid oz. triple sec

Direction

- Fill a blender with crushed ice. Pour in triple sec, limeade concentrate and tequila and blend until smooth. Transfer to glasses then serve.

106. Margaritas By The Pitcher

"Make this fantastic margarita without mixing. It tastes fabulous even if you use fairly cheap triple sec and tequila. For margaritas on the rocks, serve over ice. For margarita slushies, make several hours ahead then freeze."
Serving: 8 | Prep: 10m | Ready in: 10m

Ingredients

- 3 3/4 cups water
- 1 cup white sugar
- 1/2 cup lime juice
- 1/2 cup lemon juice
- 1 splash orange juice
- 1 1/2 cups tequila
- 3/4 cup triple sec

Direction

- In a 2-qt. pitcher, combine sugar and water together till dissolved.
- Add orange juice, lemon juice and lime juice into the pitcher then stir. Stir in triple sec and tequila.

Nutrition Information

- Calories: 288 calories;
- Total Carbohydrate: 38.4 g
- Cholesterol: 0 mg
- Total Fat: 0.1 g
- Protein: 0.1 g
- Sodium: 6 mg

107. Margaritas Maravillosos

""I like drinking my margarita over ice and in a glass without salt on its rim.""
Serving: 5 | Prep: 15m | Ready in: 15m

Ingredients

- 1 (12 oz.) can frozen limeade concentrate
- 10 (1.5 fluid oz.) jiggers gold tequila
- 5 (1.5 fluid oz.) jiggers triple sec

- 2 tbsps. fresh lime juice
- 1 tbsp. freshly grated lime peel
- 4 tsps. white sugar
- 5 cups ice

Direction

- In a blender, blend the lime juice, sugar, lime zest, tequila, frozen limeade concentrate, and triple sec until well-mixed. Pour it in a glass filled with ice. You can also add ice cubes into the margarita mix and blend the mixture until slushy; pour it into the glasses to serve.

Nutrition Information

- Calories: 584 calories;
- Total Carbohydrate: 78.4 g
- Cholesterol: 0 mg
- Total Fat: 0.1 g
- Protein: 0.1 g
- Sodium: 11 mg

108. Margaritas On The Rocks

"This is the recipe for you to make the best batch of margaritas ever."
Serving: 8 | Prep: 10m | Ready in: 10m

Ingredients

- 2 cups sweet and sour mix
- 1 cup triple sec
- 1 1/2 cups gold tequila
- 1/3 cup brandy-based orange liqueur (such as Grand Marnier®)
- 2 limes, quartered

Direction

- Pour over a small plate with salt. Use lime to rub on the glasses' rims and salt by pressing them into the plate of salt. Add ice to fill the glasses.
- Combine Grand Marnier, tequila, triple sec, sour and sweet mix in a blender. Process till smooth. Transfer into glasses and squeeze in each glass with a quarter lime. Serve.

109. Margaritas To Die For

"This drink will worth your work."
Serving: 4 | Prep: 20m | Ready in: 1day20m

Ingredients

- 2 limes
- 1/4 cup white sugar
- 3 tbsps. water
- 1 cup premium tequila
- 2 tbsps. brandy-based orange liqueur (such as Grand Marnier®)
- 1 lime, sliced into rounds
- coarse salt

Direction

- In a small bowl, grate the zest from 2 limes. Halve the zested lime. Squeeze to get 1/2 measuring cup of juice. Combine water, sugar, lime juice and lime zest. Store in the fridge, covered, for approximately 24 hours.
- Stir in Grand Marnier and tequila before serving. Rub sliced lime on the rim of 4 glasses then dip the rim into salt. Halve another slice of lime then cut under skin to halfway point of the lime to garnish the glass.

110. Margaritas With A Bite

"As a great present for your family for hot summer days, these margaritas melt slowly staying nice and COLD!""
Serving: 4 | Prep: 7m | Ready in: 7m

Ingredients

- 8 (1.5 fluid oz.) jiggers gold tequila
- 4 (1.5 fluid oz.) jiggers triple sec
- 3/4 (12 fluid oz.) can frozen limeade concentrate
- 4 cups ice

Direction

- Combine tequila, limeade concentrate and triple sec in a blender. Fill ice over the top. Pour additional ice while blending, blend until thick and smooth. Strain into glasses and serve.

111. Marge's Margaritas

""This margarita is best when served in a salt-rimmed glass together with a slice of lemon or lime.""
Serving: 8 | Prep: 10m | Ready in: 10m

Ingredients

- 1 (12 oz.) can frozen lemonade concentrate
- 12 fluid oz. tequila
- 1 cup ice cubes, or as needed
- 6 fluid oz. triple sec
- 2 tsps. lemon juice

Direction

- In a blender, blend the lemon juice, triple sec, tequila, lemonade, and ice cubes until you reached its desired thickness.

Nutrition Information

- Calories: 277 calories;
- Total Carbohydrate: 35.8 g
- Cholesterol: 0 mg
- Total Fat: 0.2 g
- Protein: 0.2 g
- Sodium: 5 mg

112. Melon Lime Slushy

"A frosty drink that is refreshing as frozen lemonade. This drink is also added with lushness of summer melon and the fruit's sweetness will have some grown-up dimension with the fresh thyme."
Serving: Makes 4 servings

Ingredients

- 6 cups diced honeydew, cantaloupe or watermelon
- 1/4 cup fresh lime juice, plus more to taste
- 1/2 cup sugar, plus more to taste
- 1 tsp. fresh thyme leaves, plus sprigs for garnish
- 1/2 cup silver tequila or mezcal (optional)

Direction

- Place melon pieces in a single layer on a rimmed baking sheet. Freeze for 1 hour till just hard.
- In a food processor, place melon pieces and add tequila (if preferred), 1/2 cup of water, thyme, sugar and lime juice. Pulse till slushy and smooth, occasionally scrap the bowl's sides. For a thinner consistency, add water if you want. Seasoning with sugar and lime juice.
- Transfer into serving glasses and add thyme sprig for garnish. Use spoons to serve immediately or serve as a drink by allow it to melt slightly.

113. Mexicali Beer Margaritas

"A delicious beer margarita with an extra hit."
Serving: 6 | Prep: 5m | Ready in: 5m

Ingredients

- 1 (12 fluid oz.) can limeade concentrate
- 1 1/2 cups gold tequila
- 3 (12 fluid oz.) cans Mexican beer
- 1 whole lime, cut into 6 wedges

Direction

- In a pitcher, put beer, tequila and limeade; mix. Fill tall glasses using ice. Put mixture into glasses. Squeeze a wedge of lime into every drink.

114. Mexican Coffee Cocktail

"Mexico makes its own spiked coffee by adding quite a kick to this warming drink using tequila and coffee liqueur."
Serving: 1 | Prep: 5m | Ready in: 5m

Ingredients

- 1 fluid oz. coffee-flavored liqueur (such as Kahlua®)
- 1/2 fluid oz. tequila
- 5 fluid oz. hot coffee
- 2 tbsps. whipped cream

Direction

- In a coffee cup, combine tequila and coffee liqueur. Add coffee and place whipped cream on top.

Nutrition Information

- Calories: 155 calories;
- Total Carbohydrate: 12 g
- Cholesterol: 5 mg
- Total Fat: 1.4 g
- Protein: 0.2 g
- Sodium: 11 mg

115. Mexican Martinis

""Don't forget to use a decent lime squeezer and fresh limes. This drink is worth a try!""
Serving: 2 | Prep: 10m | Ready in: 10m

Ingredients

- 4 limes, juiced
- coarse salt
- 2 jalapeno-stuffed green olives
- 2 (1.5 fluid oz.) jiggers premium tequila
- 1 (1.5 fluid oz.) jigger orange liqueur
- 1 (1.5 fluid oz.) jigger sweetened lime juice
- 1/2 tsp. superfine sugar
- crushed ice

Direction

- Use a little of lime juice to moisten the edges of the two martini glasses. Press the moistened edges into the coarse salt. Put an olive on each of the glasses.
- In a cocktail shaker, combine the remaining lime juice, orange liqueur, tequila, sugar, and sweetened lime juice. Fill the shaker with ice and shake it vigorously. Strain the drink into the prepared glasses.

116. Mexican Seafood Sauté With Avocado-mango Salsa

"This impressive main course pairs shrimp and sautéed scallops with a vibrant sweet-savory salsa. Serve flour tortillas or warm corn together with the side dishes and the seafood."
Serving: Makes 6 servings

Ingredients

- 1 mango, peeled, pitted, diced (about 1 1/2 cups)
- 1 large avocado, peeled, pitted, diced
- 1 large shallot, chopped (about 1/4 cup)
- 1 jalapeño chile, seeded, finely chopped (about 1 1/2 tbsps.)
- 2 tbsps. finely chopped fresh mint
- 2 tbsps. fresh lime juice
- 1/3 cup chopped shallots (about 2 medium)
- 1/4 cup fresh lime juice
- 1/4 cup tequila
- 2 garlic cloves, pressed
- 2 tsps. ground cumin
- 1/3 cup plus 4 tbsps. olive oil, divided
- 1 1/2 lbs. uncooked jumbo shrimp, peeled, deveined

- 1 lb. sea scallops, side muscles removed
- 12 green onions, thinly sliced (white and pale green parts only; about 1 1/2 cups)
- Lime slices

Direction

- To make salsa: In a medium bowl, combine all the ingredients. Add salt to taste. Let chill, covered. You can make this 2 hours ahead and keep it chilled.
- To prepare seafood: In a small bowl, whisk the initial 5 ingredients till blended. Whisk in slowly 1/3 cup of olive oil. Add pepper and salt into the marinade to taste.
- Place shrimp and scallops in two separate large resealable plastic bags. Add marinade into bags equally, about 1/2 cup for each bag. Seal bags then turn till coated. Let chill for at least 30 minutes and no more than 1 hour.
- Drain scallops and shrimp. Boil marinade in a small saucepan and put aside.
- Pat dry the scallops. In a heavy large skillet, heat 2 tbsp. of oil over medium-high heat. Sauté scallops in a skillet for 1 1/2 minutes each side till they begin to turn brown. Place in a large bowl. Sauté green onions and shrimp with the leftover 2 tbsp. of oil in the skillet for 3 minutes, stirring often till the center of the shrimp is almost opaque. Bring scallops and any accumulated juices back to the skillet. Simmer with the boiled marinade for 1-2 minutes till the mixture is heated through and it's just opaque in the seafood's center. Place into a large shallow bowl and add lime slices to garnish. Serve the dish with salsa.
- For the drink: Mexican beer matches naturally with this dish. You can choose Bohemia for its refreshment, crispy and slight spiciness.

Nutrition Information

- Calories: 455
- Total Carbohydrate: 19 g
- Cholesterol: 161 mg
- Total Fat: 29 g
- Fiber: 5 g
- Protein: 27 g

- Sodium: 951 mg
- Saturated Fat: 4 g

117. Mexican Tuna Tostadas

"A spicy snack that tastes better than nachos. There's also a hefty 10gr of heart-healthy fat from the tuna and avocado."
Serving: Makes 8 servings

Ingredients

- 8 corn tortillas (6 inches each)
- 3 tbsps. canola oil
- 3/4 tsp. salt
- 1/2 tsp. finely chopped chipotle pepper
- 2 tbsps. fresh lime juice
- 1 tbsp. tequila
- 1/2 tsp. adobo sauce
- 1/2 tsp. ground cumin
- 1/4 tsp. sugar
- 1 lb. sushi-grade tuna, cut into 1/4-inch cubes
- 1 avocado, cut into 1/4-inch cubes
- 3 scallions (green part only), thinly sliced
- 3 tbsps. hulled pumpkin seeds

Direction

- Heat the oven to 350°F. Use a 3-in. cookie cutter to cut each tortilla into 2 rounds. Brush 1 tbsp. of oil and drizzle 1/2 tsp of salt onto both sides of tortillas. Place 1 layer of rounds on cookie sheets then bake for 10-12 minutes till crispy and edges turn golden in color. Take away from the oven. In a bowl, whisk together the leftover 1/4 tsp of salt, sugar, cumin, adobo sauce, tequila, lime juice, the leftover 2 tbsp. of oil and chipotle. In a separate bowl, place 2 tbsp. of pumpkin seeds, 2/3 of scallions, avocado and tuna. Spread over the top with the dressing and stir gently till coated, try not to let the avocado break up. On tortilla rounds, place tuna mixture then add the leftover 1/3 of scallions and the leftover 1 tbsp. of pumpkin seeds on top.

118. Mexican-style Coffee

"A mix of warm coffee with coffee liqueur and tequila."
Serving: 1 | Prep: 5m | Ready in: 5m

Ingredients

- 4 fluid oz. hot brewed coffee
- 1 fluid oz. coffee liqueur
- 1 fluid oz. tequila
- 1 tbsp. whipped topping (optional)
- 1 pinch ground cinnamon, for garnish (optional)
- 1 pinch cocoa powder, for garnish (optional)

Direction

- In a mug, add coffee then stir in tequila and coffee liqueur. Add cocoa powder, cinnamon and whipped topping to garnish.

119. Mommy's Lemonade (margaritas)

""This recipe is so quick and easy to prepare and so fit to serve for get-togethers. I always get positive reviews because of this one.""
Serving: 12 | Prep: 5m | Ready in: 35m

Ingredients

- 1 (12 fluid oz.) can frozen limeade concentrate (such as Minute Maid®), thawed
- 3 (12 fluid oz.) cans cold water
- 1 (12 fluid oz.) can tequila (such as Cuervo® Especial)
- 1/2 (12 fluid oz.) can brandy-based orange liqueur (such as Grand Marnier®)
- ice cubes
- kosher salt for rimming glasses (optional)
- 1 lime, cut into wedges (optional)

Direction

- In a pitcher, pour in limeade concentrate. Fill the can with cold water and pour it into the pitcher. Do the same steps twice to have a total of 3 cans of water. Pour tequila into the can and pour it into the pitcher. Pour orange liqueur into the can, filling it halfway, and pour the liqueur into the pitcher. Mix well. Let it chill thoroughly. Serve the drink in a salt-rimmed glass filled with ice and with a lime wedge.

Nutrition Information

- Calories: 207 calories;
- Total Carbohydrate: 29.5 g
- Cholesterol: 0 mg
- Total Fat: 0.1 g
- Protein: 0 g
- Sodium: 38 mg

120. Mr. Big's White Sangria

"A great refreshing drink for summer parties."
Serving: 13 | Prep: 15m | Ready in: 6h15m

Ingredients

- 3 oranges, thinly sliced
- 4 lemons, thinly sliced
- 4 limes, thinly sliced
- 1 1/2 cups white sugar
- 1/2 cup tequila
- 2 trays ice cubes, or as needed
- 1 (750 milliliter) bottle dry white wine
- 1 (750 milliliter) bottle champagne
- 2 cups club soda

Direction

- In a big punch bowl put lime slices, lemon slices and orange slices. Put sugar on top of the fruit. Pour in tequila, using a wooden spoon stir lightly. Submerge for 6 hours to overnight.
- In a punch bowl, put generous amount of ice. Add club soda, champagne and white wine in the ice. Mix, serve right away.

Nutrition Information

- Calories: 218 calories;
- Total Carbohydrate: 32 g
- Cholesterol: 0 mg
- Total Fat: 0.1 g
- Protein: 0.6 g
- Sodium: 10 mg

---

121. Mrs. Baxton's Long Island Iced Tea

"Make the best Long Island Iced Tea using this recipe."
Serving: 1 | Prep: 10m | Ready in: 10m

Ingredients

- 1 fluid oz. vodka
- 1 fluid oz. gold tequila
- 1 fluid oz. rum
- 1 fluid oz. gin
- 1 fluid oz. Cointreau or triple sec
- 5 fluid oz. sweet and sour mix
- 2 fluid oz. cola
- 1 lime wedge

Direction

- Put ice in a cocktail shaker until full. Add in sweet and sour mix, vodka, Cointreau, tequila, gin, and rum; cover and shake until the outside of shaker is ice-cold. In a highball glass, put in a couple of ice cubes; filter in iced tea. Add cola on top and place a lime wedge to garnish.

---

122. Nacho Vidal

"This pitcher-friendly cocktail has a refreshing quality thanks to the perfectly and spicy tart shrub with flavored drinking vinegar."
Serving: Makes 8 servings | Prep: 25m

Ingredients

- 2 limes, halved
- 3/4 cup apple cider vinegar
- 3/4 cup sugar
- 2 tbsps. honey
- 1 1/2 tsp. crushed red pepper flakes
- 2 cups tequila blanco
- 1 1/2 cups Campari
- 3/4 cup fresh lemon juice
- 3/4 cup fresh lime juice
- 8 lime wedges (for serving)

Direction

- To make chile-lime shrub: In a medium saucepan, boil all the ingredients. Lower heat and simmer for 8-10 minutes till reduced slightly. Cool and strain into a jar. Let chill, covered.
- To make assembly: In a large pitcher, combine shrub, lime juice, lemon juice, Campari and tequila.
- In a cocktail shaker, add 1 1/2 cups of tequila mixture then add ice to fill. Shake for 30 seconds till frosty. Transfer the drink into 2 rocks ice-filled glasses. Add a lime wedge to each glass for garnish. Do the same process for 3 more times.
- You can make the tequila mixture 6 hours ahead. Let chill, covered.

Nutrition Information

- Calories: 335
- Total Carbohydrate: 29 g
- Total Fat: 0 g
- Fiber: 1 g
- Protein: 0 g
- Sodium: 4 mg

- Saturated Fat: 0 g

123. Orange And Cinnamon Tequila Shot

"The recipe that you'd tell the world."
Serving: 1 | Prep: 5m | Ready in: 5m

Ingredients

- 1 slice orange, seeds removed
- 1 pinch ground cinnamon, or more to taste
- 1 (1.5 fluid oz.) jigger tequila

Direction

- Use the forefinger and thumb of your left hand to hold an orange slice. Lick the skin lining right below the left hand's thumb and drizzle with a pinch of cinnamon. Keep shot of tequila in your right hand. Lick the cinnamon, drink the shot then bite the orange slice.

Nutrition Information

- Calories: 106 calories;
- Total Carbohydrate: 2.5 g
- Cholesterol: 0 mg
- Total Fat: 0 g
- Protein: 0.2 g
- Sodium: < 1 mg

124. Orange Tequila Rickey

Serving: Serves 1

Ingredients

- 1 jigger (1 1/2 oz.) light tequila
- 1 tbsp. Grand Marnier
- 1/2 lime
- Chilled club soda or seltzer

Direction

- Combine Grand Marnier and tequila in a tall glass full of ice cubes. Squeeze over the drink with lime and let the lime drop into the glass. Add club soda to top off the drink.

125. Otter Pops® Margarita

"Use an Otter Pops® to make this amazing cocktail. You can even serve different flavors of this drink to your guests to have a festive party."
Serving: 1 | Prep: 5m | Ready in: 5m

Ingredients

- 1 frozen ice pop (such as Otter Pops®)
- 1 cup ice cubes
- 1/2 lemon, juiced
- 2 tbsps. tequila
- 1 tbsp. triple sec
- salt to taste
- 1/4 tsp. agave nectar, or more to taste

Direction

- Toss ice pop in a blender. Stir in tequila, triple sec, lemon juice, and ice cubes. Blend the mixture until it's slushy or you reached its desired consistency. Top it with sugar and a few drops of agave nectar.

Nutrition Information

- Calories: 202 calories;
- Total Carbohydrate: 30.8 g
- Cholesterol: 0 mg
- Total Fat: 0.2 g
- Protein: 0.7 g
- Sodium: 176 mg

126. Paloma

"Mexicans love this refreshing, fruity, and light tequila cocktail. It's also a great substitute for margaritas."
Serving: 1 | Prep: 5m | Ready in: 5m

Ingredients

- 2 fluid oz. tequila
- 1 1/2 tbsps. lime juice
- 1 pinch salt
- 3 cubes ice, or as desired
- 6 fluid oz. diet grapefruit soda

Direction

- In a tall glass, mix salt, lime juice, and tequila together; put in ice. Stir in diet grapefruit soda.

Nutrition Information

- Calories: 137 calories;
- Total Carbohydrate: 1.9 g
- Cholesterol: 0 mg
- Total Fat: 0 g
- Protein: 0.1 g
- Sodium: 29 mg

127. Pan Galactic Gargle Blaster

"The best alcoholic drink in the cosmos."
Serving: 2 | Prep: 10m | Ready in: 10m

Ingredients

- 1 sugar cube
- 1 drop bitters
- 1/4 tsp. salt
- 1 3/4 tsps. warm water
- 3 fluid oz. gin
- 2 fluid oz. tequila
- 1 lemon-lime-flavored immune support effervescent tablet (such as Emergen-C®)
- 1 fluid oz. peppermint schnapps
- crushed ice, as desired
- 1 olive

Direction

- In a small vessel, put in a sugar cube and top with bitters. Let it immerse to make an Algolian suntiger tooth.
- To make the Santraginus V sea water, mix water and salt together in a concave apparatus.
- In a serving glass, mix tequila (O'l Janx Spirit), gin (Arcturan Mega-gin), and the Santraginus V sea water together; drop in the effervescent tablet (Fallion marsh gas). Over the back of the spoon set above the liquid's surface, pour in the Qualactin Hypermint.
- Pour into the concoction the Algolian Suntiger tooth and allow it to dissolve. Mix in ice (Zamphuor) until the temperature hits 0°C or 32°F. Add an olive on top. Drink carefully.

Nutrition Information

- Calories: 237 calories;
- Total Carbohydrate: 8.2 g
- Cholesterol: 0 mg
- Total Fat: 0.3 g
- Protein: 0 g
- Sodium: 315 mg

128. Pangalactic Gargleblaster

"Let's try this potent drink."
Serving: 1 | Prep: 5m | Ready in: 5m

Ingredients

- 1 tbsp. gin
- 1 tbsp. light rum
- 1 tbsp. vodka
- 1 tbsp. tequila
- 2 tbsps. creme de menthe liqueur
- 2 tbsps. Galliano
- 1 cup ice cubes
- 1 slice lemon

- In the container of a blender, place the gin, vodka, crème de menthe, tequila, Galliano, rum and ice to combine, covered, blend until slushy. Strain into a glass and garnish a slice of lemon.

---

129. Papaya Margarita

"This is the perfect drink during the summer. The grated lime zest really brings the taste to another level."
Serving: Makes 4 servings

Ingredients

- 1 cup sugar
- 1/2 cup plus 2 tbsps. fresh lime juice, plus zest for garnish
- 1 1/2 tsp. minced fresh rosemary
- 1/2 large Mexican papaya, seeded, or 1 large Hawaiian papaya, halved, seeded
- 3/4 cup tequila blanco
- 4 fresh orchid blossoms (optional)

Direction

- In a saucepan, boil a cup of water and sugar for 2 minutes and stir until sugar dissolves. Transfer half a cup of the syrup to a big pitcher. Add in half a cup of cold water and lime juice. Set syrup aside. Pour the left half cup of hot syrup in a bowl and add in rosemary. Let it steep for 15 minutes. Strain rosemary syrup with a fine-mesh sieve in the lime syrup. Remove all the solids. This syrup can be made a day in advance. Just cover and keep chilled.
- Put papaya flesh in a food processor then puree until it becomes smooth. Add 3/4 cup of the puree to the pitcher with rosemary-lime syrup. Keep the leftover puree for another use. Add in tequila and whisk until blended.
- Take 4 big wine glasses and fill each with ice. Pour in the cocktail and garnish with optional orchids and zest.

Nutrition Information

- Calories: 332
- Total Carbohydrate: 61 g
- Total Fat: 0 g
- Fiber: 2 g
- Protein: 0 g
- Sodium: 9 mg
- Saturated Fat: 0 g

---

130. Parker's Famous Margaritas

""My father-in-law discovered a margarita that is made from scratch. After how many decades, he came up with this delicious recipe of ultimate Mexican cocktail.""
Serving: 4 | Prep: 5m | Ready in: 5m

Ingredients

- 5 fluid oz. tequila
- 3 fluid oz. fresh lime juice
- 1 fluid oz. sweetened lime juice
- 3 fluid oz. triple sec (orange-flavored liqueur)
- ice cubes
- 1 lime, cut into wedges
- rimming salt

Direction

- Measure the triple sec, tequila, sweetened lime juice, and lime juice into the cocktail shaker. Add a generous scoop of ice and cover it. Shake for 30 seconds until the shaker is frosty.
- Use a lime wedge to rub the rim of the margarita glass. Dip the rim into the salt. Fill the glass with ice. Strain the drink equally into the prepared glasses. Serve with a lime wedge garnished on it.

"If you don't have available fresh passion fruit, replace with the strained fresh passion-fruit puree by frozen 3 cups of passion-fruit nectar in ice cube tray. Omit the ice cubes when ready to blend."
Serving: Serves 4.

Ingredients

- 1 lb. fresh passion fruit (about 12)
- 3 cups ice cubes
- 3/4 cup white tequila
- 1/4 cup sugar

Direction

- Cut passion fruits in half then scoop seeds and pulp into a blender. Briefly blend pulp. There should still be large pieces of seeds. Through a fine sieve, force fruit into a measuring cup and remove solids. Blend 1/2 cup puree together with the leftover ingredients in a blender till smooth. Transfer drink to 4 stemmed glasses.

Nutrition Information

- Calories: 255
- Total Carbohydrate: 39 g
- Total Fat: 1 g
- Fiber: 12 g
- Protein: 2 g
- Sodium: 39 mg
- Saturated Fat: 0 g

132. Patron® Mojito

"This is a delicious twist on the classic mojito."
Serving: 1 | Prep: 5m | Ready in: 5m

Ingredients

- 2 fluid oz. silver tequila (such as Patron®)
- 12 leaves mint
- 1 tbsp. white sugar
- 3 lime wedges

- 1/4 cup club soda, or as needed

Direction

- Mix lime wedges, sugar, tequila, and mint leaves in a tall glass. Vigorously mix the mixture while crushing the mint using back of a spoon to release the oils and press juice from lemon wedges. Add club soda on top, mix gently and serve.

Nutrition Information

- Calories: 184 calories;
- Total Carbohydrate: 14.1 g
- Cholesterol: 0 mg
- Total Fat: 0 g
- Protein: 0.1 g
- Sodium: 3 mg

133. Peachy Keen Long Island Iced Tea

"This cocktail is just like a Long Island but with a delicious twist. You can halve this recipe to serve in a double tall bar glass."
Serving: 1 | Prep: 10m | Ready in: 10m

Ingredients

- 1 fluid oz. peach schnapps
- 1 fluid oz. vodka
- 1 fluid oz. gin
- 1 fluid oz. gold tequila
- 1 fluid oz. rum
- 3 fluid oz. sweet and sour mix
- 1 fluid oz. cola, or to taste

Direction

- Put ice in a big glass and fill; add in rum, peach schnapps, tequila, vodka, and gin. Mix in sweet and sour mix. Add a splash of cola on top then mix.

Nutrition Information

- Calories: 566 calories;

- Total Carbohydrate: 52.5 g
- Cholesterol: 0 mg
- Total Fat: 0.1 g
- Protein: 0 g
- Sodium: 5 mg

134. Peachy Orange Surprise

"After a long hard day of work, this drink is sure to help you unwind and refresh you."
Serving: 1 | Prep: 5m | Ready in: 5m

Ingredients

- 1 fluid oz. grenadine syrup
- 1 cup crushed ice, or as needed
- 1/2 fluid oz. white tequila
- 1/2 fluid oz. white rum
- 1/4 cup peach juice, or as needed
- 1/4 cup orange juice, or as needed
- 1 sprig mint

Direction

- Place grenadine onto a hurricane glass' bottom. Add crushed ice to fill 2/3 of the glass. Pour in rum and tequila. Add equal amounts of orange juice and peach to top off. Add mint to garnish.

Nutrition Information

- Calories: 228 calories;
- Total Carbohydrate: 40.5 g
- Cholesterol: 0 mg
- Total Fat: 0.2 g
- Protein: 0.7 g
- Sodium: 23 mg

135. Persimmon Margarita

"One thing that I love to do whenever there are persimmons is to press the ripe fruit through a fine-mesh strainer, discarding the seeds and skin, and shake well to come up with my version of fall Margaritas."
Serving: Serves 1

Ingredients

- 2 oz. reposado tequila
- 2 oz. Paula's Texas Orange
- 2 oz. persimmon puree
- 1 oz. freshly squeezed lime juice
- Cinnamon-Sugar-Cayenne Rim

Direction

- Mix all the liquid ingredients in a mixing glass. Put in ice and shake them vigorously until chilled and emulsified. Strain the drink into a pint glass filled with ice. Make sure that the glass is rimmed with the cinnamon-sugar-cayenne rim.

Nutrition Information

- Calories: 238
- Total Carbohydrate: 29 g
- Total Fat: 0 g
- Fiber: 2 g
- Protein: 1 g
- Sodium: 2 mg
- Saturated Fat: 0 g

136. Pineapple-hibiscus Cocktail

"You'll love the citrusy sour flavor and the amazing color of hibiscus."
Serving: Makes 8

Ingredients

- 1 1/4 cups sugar
- 1 pineapple, peeled, cut into 1 1/2-inch pieces
- 6 tbsps. distilled white vinegar
- 1/4 cup dried hibiscus flowers

- 1 jalapeño, thinly sliced into rounds
- 5 sprigs mint
- 1 lime, thinly sliced into wheels
- 2 cups tequila
- 1 cup fresh lime juice

Direction

- Boil 1 cup of water and sugar in a medium saucepan. Cook and stir for 3 minutes till sugar is dissolved. Place in pineapple, lower heat, simmer for 10 minutes. Take away from the heat then allow to sit till the pineapple flavor is infused with the syrup, for 30 minutes. In a small bowl, strain the mixture; add in vinegar and stir. Chill the shrub, covered, for 30 minutes till cold. Chill the pineapple pieces, covered, till ready to use.
- In the meantime, in a small bowl, add hibiscus and pour over with 1 1/4 cups of boiling water. Cover then allow to steep for 10 minutes. In an airtight container, strain the tea and remove the flowers. Cover and let the tea chill for 30 second till cold.
- Put aside 8 pieces of pineapple and 8 slices of jalapeño for serving. In a large pitcher, stir 1 cup of tea, 1 cup of shrub, the leftover pineapple and jalapeño, lime juice, tequila, lime wheels and mint. Let chill for at least 60 minutes.
- Serve in rock glasses that are filled with ice with the reserved pineapple pieces and jalapeño slices for garnish.
- You can mix the cocktail 6 hours ahead and keep it chilled.

137. Pink Cadillac Margarita

"This is a refreshing change from a traditional margarita."
Serving: 1 | Prep: 5m | Ready in: 5m

Ingredients

- 2 fluid oz. gold tequila
- 2 fluid oz. sweet-and-sour cocktail mix
- 1 fluid oz. orange liqueur (such as Cointreau®)

- 1 fluid oz. cranberry juice
- 1 splash orange juice
- ice cubes

Direction

- In a cocktail shaker, pour orange juice, sweet-and-sour mix, orange liqueur, cranberry juice, and tequila. Take a cover and shake vigorously until well-combined.
- Pour over ice into oversized martini glass or a tall glass.

Nutrition Information

- Calories: 374 calories;
- Total Carbohydrate: 42.1 g
- Cholesterol: 0 mg
- Total Fat: 0.1 g
- Protein: 0.1 g
- Sodium: 11 mg

138. Pink Cadillac Margaritas

"Like being at a bar."
Serving: 8 | Prep: 10m | Ready in: 10m

Ingredients

- 1 (1 liter) bottle bottled margarita mix
- 2 1/2 cups tequila (such as 1800® Premium Reposado)
- 1/2 cup orange liqueur (such as Grand Marnier®)
- 1/4 cup raspberry liqueur (such as Chambord®)
- 2 tbsps. salt, or as needed
- 2 limes, cut into wedges
- crushed ice

Direction

- In a pitcher, mix together raspberry liqueur, orange liqueur, tequila and margarita mix.
- Transfer salt onto a small and shallow plate. Use a wedge of lime to moisten 8 margarita glasses' rims. Dip the rims in salt till coated. In

each glass, squeeze some lime juice and add ice. Pour over the ice with margarita mixture.

Nutrition Information

- Calories: 245 calories;
- Total Carbohydrate: 10.1 g
- Cholesterol: 0 mg
- Total Fat: 0.1 g
- Protein: 0 g
- Sodium: 1747 mg

139. Pink Panther

"Garnish the drink with cherry, pineapple slice and umbrella to get a nice beverage to have around the pool on hot summer days."
Serving: 1 | Prep: 3m | Ready in: 3m

Ingredients

- 1 cup crushed ice
- 1 fluid oz. amaretto liqueur
- 1 fluid oz. vodka
- 8 fluid oz. pineapple juice
- 1 tsp. grenadine syrup
- 1 slice fresh pineapple
- 1 maraschino cherry

Direction

- Combine grenadine, pineapple juice, vodka, amaretto and ice together in a blender; blend well. In a tall chilled glass, pour the drink then add cherry, pineapple slice and umbrella to garnish.

140. Pitcher Perfect Margaritas

"Finally, I discovered a way to have the real margarita taste in a pitcher after twisting with a few other margarita recipes."
Serving: 8 | Prep: 10m | Ready in: 10m

Ingredients

- 2 cups tequila
- 1 cup triple sec
- 3/4 cup fresh lime juice
- 3/4 cup sweetened lime juice
- 3 cups ice
- kosher salt
- 8 lime wedges

Direction

- In a large pitcher, mix the sweetened lime juice, tequila, fresh lime juice, triple sec, and ice. Stir well.
- Transfer kosher salt onto a plate. Use a lime wedge to rub the rim of a glass. Dunk rim of the glass into the salt and then add the margarita mixture until glass is filled. Repeat this for each serving.

141. Pomegranate Margarita

""Combining fresh lime and pomegranate juice makes this drink a keeper! Give away your keys before this one hits.""
Serving: 6 | Prep: 15m | Ready in: 15m

Ingredients

- 1 cup tequila
- 1 cup triple sec
- 1/4 cup confectioners' sugar
- 4 cups ice
- 1 cup pomegranate juice
- 1 cup fresh lime juice

Direction

- In a pitcher, combine the triple sec and tequila. Sprinkle the mixture with confectioners' sugar; stir well to dissolve. Add the ice. Pour in lime juice and pomegranate juice. Stir the mixture until well-blended; serve. If you're a professional, you can add more tequila to taste.

142. Presidente Margarita

"The secret in this presidential margarita is through brandy and tequila. You'll love this!"
Serving: 1 | Prep: 5m | Ready in: 5m

Ingredients

- salt for rimming glass
- 3 cubes ice, or as desired
- 4 fluid oz. sweet-and-sour cocktail mix
- 1 1/4 fluid oz. tequila
- 1/2 fluid oz. orange-flavored liqueur (such as Cointreau®)
- 1/2 fluid oz. brandy (such as Presidente®)
- 1 splash lime juice

Direction

- Surround the rim of a margarita glass with salt. Fill the glass with ice. In a cocktail shaker, pour in brandy, orange liqueur, cocktail mix, lime juice, and tequila. Cover and shake to combine. Pour the mixture into the prepared glass.

Nutrition Information

- Calories: 416 calories;
- Total Carbohydrate: 55.4 g
- Cholesterol: 0 mg
- Total Fat: 0.1 g
- Protein: 0.1 g
- Sodium: 4 mg

143. Prickly Pear Cactus Margarita

"This cocktail recipe came from one bartender in Tucson."
Serving: 1 | Prep: 10m | Ready in: 10m

Ingredients

- coarse salt as needed
- 2 fluid oz. tequila
- 2 fluid oz. sweet and sour mix
- 1 fluid oz. triple sec
- 1 fluid oz. lime juice
- 1 fluid oz. prickly pear syrup

Direction

- Put salt in a small plate. Moisten the lip of a margarita glass; press in the plate of salt.
- Put ice in a cocktail shaker until full. Add in pear syrup, tequila, lime juice, sweet and sour mix, and triple sec; cover and shake the cocktail shaker well. Filter cocktail in the prepared margarita glass.

Nutrition Information

- Calories: 423 calories;
- Total Carbohydrate: 56.3 g
- Cholesterol: 0 mg
- Total Fat: 0.1 g
- Protein: 0.1 g
- Sodium: 3 mg

144. Prune Tequila Ice Cream

"If you are having Apple Crisp with Prune Tequila Ice Cream, then this recipe will surely complement these. Overall preparation time: 2 days (macerating and freezing included) Cooking time: 30 minutes"
Serving: Makes about 1 quart

Ingredients

- 3/4 cup prunes (dried plums; about 5 oz)
- 1/3 cup gold tequila
- 2 cups heavy cream
- 1 cup half-and-half

- 1/2 vanilla bean, split lengthwise
- 6 large egg yolks
- 1/4 cup plus 2 tbsps. sugar
- Special equipment: an ice cream maker

Direction

- Fill 1/2-pint jar with prunes and just cover tequila then cover. Set aside at room temperature and macerate prunes for at least 12 hours to soften.
- In a 2- to 3-quart heavy saucepan, combine half and half, vanilla bean and cream and bring it to a boil. In a bowl, whisk yolks and sugar together then in a stream pour the hot cream mixture in while whisking. Transfer the custard in the saucepan and cook it. Make sure to set the temperature to medium-low heat and use an instant thermometer to keep the temperature in check. Stir until the temperature turns 170 to 175°F and pour the custard promptly into a bowl through a mesh strainer. Stir from time to time, letting it cool to a room temperature. Cover it and chill for another 4 hours.
- Pour the macerated prunes (liquid included) in a food processor. Pulse until becomes a slightly thick and chunky puree and add 1 cup of chilled custard. Pulse until blended, pour it back in the rest of the custard and whisk.
- Use an ice cream maker to freeze the custard then transfer it into a sealed container. Set it in freezer for at least 12 hours to harden. The Ice cream will be softer than normal due to the tequila added with the prunes.
- You can macerate the prunes for up to 1 week and make the ice cream 3 days ahead.

Nutrition Information

- Calories: 258
- Total Carbohydrate: 16 g
- Cholesterol: 154 mg
- Total Fat: 19 g
- Protein: 3 g
- Sodium: 28 mg
- Saturated Fat: 11 g

145. Purple And Gold Margarita

"Sour mix shaken up with raspberry liqueur and gold tequila."
Serving: 1 | Prep: 2m | Ready in: 2m

Ingredients

- 1 (1.5 fluid oz.) jigger gold tequila
- 1/2 cup sweet and sour mix
- 1 (1.5 fluid oz.) jigger raspberry flavored liqueur

Direction

- Pour over a small plate with salt. Use a damp towel to moisten the rim of a big margarita glass then salt the rim by pressing it into the salt.
- Combine raspberry liqueur, sour mix and tequila in an ice-filled cocktail mixture. Shake vigorously then strain the drink into the glass with salt rim.

146. Quick And Easy Mango Margaritas

""Here's the secret of my sweet and refreshing mango margaritas.""
Serving: 4 | Prep: 5m | Ready in: 5m

Ingredients

- 2 cups ice
- 12 fluid oz. margarita mix
- 6 fluid oz. tequila
- 4 fluid oz. mango nectar
- 1 lime, halved
- 1 tbsp. white sugar, or as needed

Direction

- In a blender, mix the mango nectar, margarita mix, tequila, and ice. Squeeze in 1 lime half. Blend the mixture until it is smooth.

- Cut the remaining lime half into wedges. In a small and shallow plate, fill it with 1/4 to 1/2-inch of sugar. Wet the rims of the 4 glasses using the lime wedge. Dip the moistened rims into the plate with sugar. Fill each glass with the cocktail.

Nutrition Information

- Calories: 208 calories;
- Total Carbohydrate: 27.4 g
- Cholesterol: 0 mg
- Total Fat: 0.1 g
- Protein: 0.2 g
- Sodium: 65 mg

147. Raspberry Margaritas

"Summer parties are perfect when you serve this drink."
Serving: 6 | Prep: 5m | Ready in: 5m

Ingredients

- 1 cup frozen unsweetened raspberries
- 1 cup brandy-based orange liqueur (such as Grand Marnier®)
- 3/4 cup gold tequila
- 1/2 cup fresh lemon juice
- 2 tbsps. superfine sugar
- ice cubes

Direction

- In a blender, blend sugar, raspberries, lemon juice, brandy-based orange liqueur, and tequila until smooth. Pour in glasses with ice cubes.

148. Raspberry Orange Margaritas

Serving: Serves 4.

Ingredients

- 2 cups (about 10 oz.) raspberries
- 3/4 cup fresh orange juice

- 3/4 cup white tequila
- 2 tbsps. sugar

Direction

- In a blender, puree the raspberries. Force the puree to a small bowl through a fine sieve and remove solids. Combine the rest of the ingredients with 1/2 cup of puree in a cocktail shaker. Shake well then transfer the drink into a tall glass filled with ice.

Nutrition Information

- Calories: 178
- Total Carbohydrate: 20 g
- Total Fat: 1 g
- Fiber: 5 g
- Protein: 1 g
- Sodium: 2 mg
- Saturated Fat: 0 g

149. Refreshing Watermelon Margarita

"Combat hot summer nights with this refreshing cocktail."
Serving: 2 | Prep: 10m | Ready in: 3h10m

Ingredients

- 1/2 watermelon, cubed
- 3/4 cup tequila
- 1/4 cup lime juice
- 1/4 cup white sugar

Direction

- In a blender, process watermelon until smooth. Strain in a fine mesh strainer to get rid of the pump and seeds.
- Transfer watermelon juice in a tray of ice cube; place in freezer for 3hrs until frozen.
- In a blender, process sugar, four cups of frozen watermelon cubes, lime juice, and tequila together until smooth.

Nutrition Information

- Calories: 403 calories;
- Total Carbohydrate: 53.3 g
- Cholesterol: 0 mg
- Total Fat: 0.5 g
- Protein: 2.2 g
- Sodium: 5 mg

150. Rhubarb Margarita

""I like serving this sweet-tart combination of a drink on a hot day.""
Serving: 4 | Prep: 10m | Ready in: 2h30m

Ingredients

- 4 cups diced rhubarb
- 1/2 cup water
- 1/2 cup white sugar
- 4 cups ice
- 2/3 cup tequila

Direction

- Place the rhubarb and water in a saucepan. Cover the saucepan and let it simmer over medium heat. Adjust the heat to medium-low. Let it simmer for 15 more minutes until the rhubarb starts to break down and release all of its juice. Strain its juice and squeeze the pulp to squeeze out the liquid as much as you can. Discard the pulp after squeezing it. Mix sugar with the hot juice. Refrigerate the syrup for at least 2 hours until it's very cold.
- Fill the blender with ice to prepare for the margarita. Pour in rhubarb syrup and tequila. Blend the mixture until it is smooth or until you reached its desired consistency. Pour the mixture into the margarita glasses. Serve.

Nutrition Information

- Calories: 210 calories;
- Total Carbohydrate: 30.5 g
- Cholesterol: 0 mg
- Total Fat: 0.2 g

- Protein: 1.1 g
- Sodium: 13 mg

151.Riverbank Margaritas

"Enjoy the riverbank margaritas! Very tasty!"
Serving: 8 | Prep: 5m | Ready in: 5m

Ingredients

- 1 (12 fluid oz.) can frozen limeade concentrate
- 12 fluid oz. tequila
- 1 (12 fluid oz.) can or bottle lemon-lime soda (such as Sprite®)
- 1 (12 fluid oz.) can or bottle Mexican beer

Direction

- In a pitcher, combine limeade, beer, tequila, and lemon-lime soda together.

Nutrition Information

- Calories: 271 calories;
- Total Carbohydrate: 40.4 g
- Cholesterol: 0 mg
- Total Fat: 0 g
- Protein: 0.2 g
- Sodium: 7 mg

152. Romulan Margarita

""The coating of the rim with salt is optional. No need to ask how I came up with this recipe.""
Serving: 4 | Prep: 5m | Ready in: 5m

Ingredients

- 3/4 cup tequila
- 1/2 cup blue curacao liqueur
- 1 tsp. lime juice
- ice

Direction

- In a 2-cup measuring cup, mix the blue curacao liqueur, lime juice, and tequila. Pour the mixture in a margarita pitcher filled with ice. If desired, you can also blend the mixture in a blender filled with ice to a slush. Serve the drink in a margarita glass.

Nutrition Information

- Calories: 211 calories;
- Total Carbohydrate: 14.2 g
- Cholesterol: 0 mg
- Total Fat: 0.1 g
- Protein: 0 g
- Sodium: 4 mg

153. Rosy Boa Cocktail

"The special thing about this cocktail is the rose water."
Serving: 8 servings

Ingredients

- 1 tbsp. kosher salt
- 2 tsps. paprika
- 1 tsp. chipotle chile powder
- 2 cups fresh grapefruit juice
- 1 1/2 cups tequila
- 1/2 cup pomegranate juice
- 1/3 cup fresh lime juice
- 1/4 tsp. rose water
- 1 1/2 cups (or more) ginger beer
- Grapefruit wedges (for serving)

Direction

- In a small bowl, combine chile powder, paprika and salt. Get 8 rocks glasses then moisten and dip 1/2 of each of their rim into chile salt. Put the glasses aside.
- In an 8-cup measuring glass or a large pitcher, combine rose water, lime juice, pomegranate juice, tequila and grapefruit juice. Stir in 1 cup of ice till the cocktail is the very cold and ice melts. Add in ginger beer and stir. Add ice to fill the prepped glasses then pour the cocktail into glasses. Add grapegfruit wedges to garnish and place more ginger beer on top, if preferred.
- You can make the grapefruit mixture 8 hours ahead. Add in ice, stir, cover and let chill. Place ginger beer into the prepped glasses right before serving.

Nutrition Information

- Calories: 149
- Total Carbohydrate: 13 g
- Total Fat: 0 g
- Fiber: 0 g
- Protein: 1 g
- Sodium: 409 mg
- Saturated Fat: 0 g

154. Ruby Red Margarita

Serving: Serves 1

Ingredients

- 1 lime wedge
- Coarse salt for coating the rim of the glass
- 1 jigger (1 1/2 oz.) tequila
- 3 tbsps. fresh pink grapefruit juice (preferably ruby red)
- 1 pony (1 oz.) orange-flavored liqueur
- 1/2 tsp. superfine sugar if desired
- Garnish: 1 quarter of a slice of ruby red grapefruit

Direction

- Use a lime wedge to rub the cocktail glass's rim. Lightly dip and coat the rim in salt. Chill the glass.
- Blend 1 cup of ice cubes, sugar, liqueur, grapefruit juice and tequila for 30 seconds in a blender. Transfer the drink to the glass and add grapefruit slice for garnish.

Nutrition Information

- Calories: 301
- Total Carbohydrate: 31 g
- Total Fat: 0 g
- Fiber: 0 g
- Protein: 0 g
- Sodium: 352 mg
- Saturated Fat: 0 g

155. Salsa Borracha

"This "drunken" salsas use tequila instead of pilque as in the original recipe. The cooking process burns off most of the alcohol and only musky flavor left. The salsa will be balanced wonderfully with the sweetness coming from the freshly squeezed orange juice."
Serving: Makes 1 cup

Ingredients

- 8 ancho chiles
- 1/2 cup fresh orange juice
- 1/2 cup golden tequila
- 1 garlic clove, minced
- 4 tbsps. olive oil
- Salt and freshly ground black pepper
- 1/4 cup crumbled añejo or feta cheese

Direction

- In a dry sauté pan, cook the chiles for 2 minutes over high heat while turning constantly till toasted slightly. Cut the chiles in half and remove the seeds. Tear the chiles into small pieces and place in a blender.
- Add 2 tbsp. of olive oil, garlic, tequila and orange juice to the blender. Puree till nearly smooth.
- In a sauté pan, heat the leftover 2 tbsp. of olive oil over high heat. Add and cook till slightly thickened for 5 minutes. Add pepper and salt to taste the salsa. Allow to cool completely. You can make the salsa the day before. Refrigerate the sauce, covered.

Nutrition Information

- Calories: 640
- Total Carbohydrate: 43 g
- Cholesterol: 17 mg
- Total Fat: 37 g
- Fiber: 15 g
- Protein: 11 g
- Sodium: 543 mg
- Saturated Fat: 7 g

156. Salty Chihuahua

"This recipe is a variation on the salty dog, called Salty Chihuahua."
Serving: 1 | Prep: 1m | Ready in: 1m

Ingredients

- 1 wedge lime
- coarse salt
- ice
- 1 (1.5 fluid oz.) jigger tequila
- 5 fluid oz. lemonade

Direction

- Use lime juice to wet an old-fashioned glass's rim then dip it in salt. Add ice to fill the glass. Pour in lemonade and tequila. Squeeze the lime wedge and let it drop in the glass. Stir.

Nutrition Information

- Calories: 176 calories;
- Total Carbohydrate: 19.2 g
- Cholesterol: 0 mg
- Total Fat: 0 g
- Protein: 0 g
- Sodium: 13 mg

157. Sangria Y Tequila Ponche (punch)

"Make your punch more festive with tequila, wine and frozen berries."
Serving: 20 | Prep: 5m | Ready in: 35m

Ingredients

- 1 (10 oz.) package frozen mixed berries, thawed
- 6 (1.5 fluid oz.) jiggers tequila
- 1 (1.5 liter) bottle chilled white Zinfandel wine
- 2 cups pineapple juice
- 1 (12 fluid oz.) can frozen lemonade concentrate, thawed
- 1 liter ginger ale

Direction

- In a punch bowl, combine tequila and berries then soak for 30 minutes.
- Add lemonade concentration, pineapple juice and wine into the tequila and berry mixture then stir. Gently stir into the bowl with ginger ale.

Nutrition Information

- Calories: 156 calories;
- Total Carbohydrate: 20.1 g
- Cholesterol: 0 mg
- Total Fat: 0.1 g
- Protein: 0.3 g
- Sodium: 11 mg

158. Screwrita

"This recipe highlights the orange juice."
Serving: 1 | Prep: 5m | Ready in: 5m

Ingredients

- 1/2 cup ice
- 1/2 cup orange juice
- 1 fluid oz. tequila
- 1/2 fluid oz. triple sec
- 1 tsp. sugar
- 1 dash fresh lime juice

Direction

- In a glass filled with ice, mix in a triple sec, lime juice, orange juice, sugar, and tequila. Mix it well.

159. Skewered Beef Fajitas

"You can serve salsa, grated cheese, guacamole, and sour cream with the fajitas. Start with Margaritas and then complete with coffee ice cream sprinkled with Kahlúa."
Serving: Makes 2 servings; can be doubled

Ingredients

- 2 tbsps. vegetable oil
- 2 tbsps. fresh lime juice
- 1 1/2 tbsps. tequila
- 2 tsps. minced jalapeño chili
- 1 tsp. grated lime peel
- 8 to 10 oz. skirt steak, cut crosswise into 1-inch-wide strips
- 6 large green onions, trimmed to 8-inch length
- 8 1-inch squares green bell pepper
- 4 6- to 7-inch-diameter flour tortillas

Direction

- Start by preparing the barbecue (medium-high heat). Then whisk the first five ingredients into an 8x8x2-inch glass baking dish to blend. Add green onions and beef, and mix to coat. Allow to stand for ten minutes. Onto two long metal skewers, thread the beef. Onto 2 long metal skewers, thread the green onions and bell pepper squares. Drizzle with pepper and salt.
- Grill the veggies and beef while flipping often for about 8 minutes until the veggies are a bit charred and almost tender and the beef is cooked to the preferred doneness. In the meantime, grill the tortillas for about one minute on each side until they are warm and starting to brown in spots. Push the veggies and beef off the skewers onto a work surface

using a fork. Then chop coarsely. Put two tortillas onto each plate. Distribute the filling among the tortillas. Then roll up before serving.

Nutrition Information

- Calories: 806
- Total Carbohydrate: 77 g
- Cholesterol: 83 mg
- Total Fat: 39 g
- Fiber: 12 g
- Protein: 39 g
- Sodium: 837 mg
- Saturated Fat: 9 g

160. Skinny Margarita With Truvia® Natural Sweetener

""This is another version of the most popular cocktail in the world, but much skinnier. You will enjoy this drink by not thinking of your sugar and calories. It also has Truvia® natural sweetener in it.""
Serving: 1

Ingredients

- 1 1/2 oz. tequila
- 3/4 oz. lime juice
- 1/4 oz. orange juice
- 3/4 oz. Truvia® Simple Syrup**
- Sea salt and lime for garnish

Direction

- Place all the ingredients in a cocktail shaker. Fill the cocktail shaker halfway with ice. Shake it thoroughly.
- In a glass filled with ice, double strain the mixture and garnish.

161. Sopa De Aguacate

"A cold soup made with avocado."
Serving: Makes about 8 cups

Ingredients

- 2 tbsps. finely chopped coriander leaves
- 1 serrano chile, seeded and minced (wear rubber gloves)
- 1 cup fresh orange juice
- 1/2 tsp. freshly grated orange zest
- 1/4 cup tequila
- 2 cups cold chicken broth
- 2 California avocados (about 1 lb.), pitted, peeled and chopped coarse
- white pepper to taste
- Garnish: 2 cups chopped, peeled seeded watermelon

Direction

- Blend 1/4 cup of orange juice with serrano and coriander in a blender till a smooth paste is formed. Blend in avocados, broth, Tequila, zest and the leftover 3/4 cup of orange juice till smooth. Through a coarse sieve, pour the mixture into a large bowl then seasoning with salt and white pepper.
- Cover and let the soup chill till cold for 2 hours.
- Top the soup with watermelon and serve.

162. Speedy Chihuahua

"Try this refreshing mix between a margarita and a greyhound."
Serving: 3 | Prep: 10m | Ready in: 10m

Ingredients

- 3 lime wedges
- kosher salt for rimming glasses
- ice cubes
- 4 fluid oz. white tequila

- 1 fluid oz. orange flavored liqueur (such as Cointreau®)
- 2 limes, juiced
- 8 fluid oz. grapefruit juice
- 3 splashes club soda

Direction

- Around the rims of 3 margarita glasses, rub a lime wedge, dipping each glass rim into salt. Fill each glass with ice cubes.
- In a pitcher, combine the tequila, grapefruit juice, lime juice, and orange liqueur together and pour the mixture into the glasses over the ice. In each glass, add 1 splash of club soda, and serve.

Nutrition Information

- Calories: 165 calories;
- Total Carbohydrate: 16.5 g
- Cholesterol: 0 mg
- Total Fat: 0.2 g
- Protein: 0.7 g
- Sodium: 137 mg

163. Spicy Grapefruit Margarita

"The tequila gets hotter the longer it is infused with chiles."
Serving: Makes 8 drinks

Ingredients

- 2 cups plus 2 tbsps. tequila
- 1-2 habanero chiles, halved
- Kosher salt
- 6 cups fresh pink grapefruit juice

Direction

- In a large pitcher, combine chiles and tequila. Allow to steep for three hours, or for longer if you want a spicier tequila. Get rid of chiles. You can prepare one month ahead, then cover and refrigerate.

- Cover a small plate with plenty of water. Onto another small plate, add plenty of salt to cover by 1/4 inch. Dunk the rims of 8 twelve-oz. glasses in the water, and then into the salt to coat lightly. Add ice until filled. Pour the grapefruit juice into the pitcher with tequila. Add ice until filled and mix until cold. Subdivide the drink into the glasses.

Nutrition Information

- Calories: 211
- Total Carbohydrate: 18 g
- Total Fat: 0 g
- Fiber: 0 g
- Protein: 1 g
- Sodium: 587 mg
- Saturated Fat: 0 g

164. Spicy Watermelon Margarita

"With just two parts of alcohol, one-part sour, and one part sweet, this simple sour mix can be a base for a lot of cocktails."
Serving: 1 | Prep: 10m | Ready in: 10m

Ingredients

- 2 cups seedless watermelon cubes
- 1 lime wedge
- 1 pinch kosher salt
- ice cubes
- 1 1/2 fluid oz. silver tequila
- 3/4 fluid oz. orange-flavored liqueur (such as Cointreau®)
- 3/4 fluid oz. lime juice
- 1 thin slice jalapeno slice, plus more for garnish
- 1 watermelon wedge

Direction

- In a blender, process watermelon until pureed. Rub a lime wedge on the rim of margarita glass then dip rim in salt.
- Place ice in a cocktail shaker, pour in two oz. of pureed watermelon, tequila, jalapeno,

orange liqueur and lime juice. Shake until the mixture is cold.

- Filter mixture in the prepared glass; add a slice of jalapeno and watermelon wedge to garnish.

Nutrition Information

- Calories: 382 calories;
- Total Carbohydrate: 63.7 g
- Cholesterol: 0 mg
- Total Fat: 1.1 g
- Protein: 4.2 g
- Sodium: 417 mg

165. Strawberry Banana Margarita

Serving: Serves 2

Ingredients

- 1 cup chopped strawberries, frozen solid
- 1 small banana
- 3 jiggers (4 1/2 oz.) tequila
- 1 jigger (1 1/2 oz.) Triple Sec
- 2 1/2 tbsps. fresh lemon juice

Direction

- Purée 1 cup of cracked ice, lemon juice, Triple sec, tequila, banana that was peeled and broken into pieces, and strawberries in a blender while occasionally scrap down the sides till the mixture is frozen but smooth. Pour the mixture into 2 stemmed glasses.

Nutrition Information

- Calories: 286
- Total Carbohydrate: 25 g
- Total Fat: 1 g
- Fiber: 3 g
- Protein: 1 g
- Sodium: 4 mg
- Saturated Fat: 0 g

166. Strawberry Basil Margarita

"This refreshing summer drink recipe is the best way to use up your basil and strawberries. Try it and enjoy it!"
Serving: 2 | Prep: 5m | Ready in: 5m

Ingredients

- 1 cup hulled strawberries
- 1/4 cup tequila
- 1 tbsp. orange-flavored liqueur, such as Cointreau ®
- 1 tbsp. lemon juice
- 2 tbsps. white sugar
- 3 large basil leaves
- 8 ice cubes

Direction

- In a blender, combine the orange-flavored liqueur, basil leaves, strawberries, lemon juice, sugar, and tequila. Blend the mixture on Low speed until smooth. Fill in ice and blend for 30-60 seconds until the ice is crushed.

167. Strawberry Beer Margaritas

"Get a flavorful twist with strawberries, mangoes or raspberries!"
Serving: 6 | Prep: 10m | Ready in: 2h10m

Ingredients

- 1 lb. fresh strawberries, hulled and cut into chunks
- 12 fluid oz. white tequila
- 1 (12 fluid oz.) can or bottle lemon-lime flavored carbonated beverage
- 1 (12 fluid oz.) can or bottle light beer
- 1 (12 fluid oz.) can frozen limeade concentrate, thawed
- ice, or as needed
- 1 tsp. kosher salt for rimming glasses (optional)

Direction

- In a bowl, place strawberry chunks. Pour in tequila over strawberries. Marinate in refrigerator for 120 minutes.
- In a blender, blend tequila and strawberries until fully pureed; remove seeds by pouring into a large pitcher.
- In a pitcher, stir strained berry mixture, limeade concentrate, soda, and beer together. Add in ice cubes to chill. Use salt to rim glasses before pouring margaritas.

Nutrition Information

- Calories: 377 calories;
- Total Carbohydrate: 58.5 g
- Cholesterol: 0 mg
- Total Fat: 0.2 g
- Protein: 0.6 g
- Sodium: 332 mg

168. Strawberry Margarita

"A refreshing summer drink."
Serving: 4 | Prep: 5m | Ready in: 5m

Ingredients

- 1 (10 oz.) package frozen strawberries
- 1 (6 oz.) can frozen pink lemonade concentrate
- 1 cup tequila
- 1/4 cup triple sec
- ice cubes

Direction

- Blend triple sec, tequila, lemonade concentrate and strawberries in a blender till smooth. Place in ice cubes as needed.

Nutrition Information

- Calories: 311 calories;
- Total Carbohydrate: 39.1 g
- Cholesterol: 0 mg
- Total Fat: 0.2 g
- Protein: 0.5 g

- Sodium: 9 mg

169. Strawberry Margarita Fizz

Serving: Makes 2 drinks

Ingredients

- Sugar for coating rims of glasses
- 1 1/2 cups softened strawberry ice cream
- 1/2 cup chopped strawberries plus whole strawberries for garnish
- 1 oz. (2 tbsps.) tequila, or to taste
- 1/2 tsp. fresh lime juice
- 1/3 cup chilled club soda
- Garnish: lime slices

Direction

- Rub water on 2 chilled stemmed glass's rims and coat by dip them in sugar.
- Blend lime juice, Tequila, chopped strawberries and ice cream in a blender till smooth but thick. Transfer into glasses. Pour in club soda. Add lime slices and whole strawberries for garnish.

Nutrition Information

- Calories: 610
- Total Carbohydrate: 127 g
- Cholesterol: 29 mg
- Total Fat: 8 g
- Fiber: 1 g
- Protein: 3 g
- Sodium: 69 mg
- Saturated Fat: 5 g

170. Strawberry Margarita Ice Pops

"Use freshly squeezed orange juice instead of the tequila to make these non-alcoholic ice pops."
Serving: Makes 8 (1/3-cup) ice pops | Prep: 10m

Ingredients

- 1 1/4 lb strawberries, hulled and halved
- 1/2 cup white tequila
- 1/2 cup superfine granulated sugar
- 1 tbsp. fresh lime juice
- 8 (1/3-cup) ice pop molds and 8 wooden sticks

Direction

- In a blender, blend all the ingredients till smooth. Force into a big glass measuring cup through a fine sieve. Transfer into molds and place in sticks.
- Store the freezer for at least 24 hours.

Nutrition Information

- Calories: 130
- Total Carbohydrate: 25 g
- Total Fat: 0 g
- Fiber: 1 g
- Protein: 0 g
- Sodium: 5 mg
- Saturated Fat: 0 g

171. Tequila And Lime Baked Pineapple

Serving: Makes 4 servings | Prep: 20m

Ingredients

- 3 tbsps. tequila (preferably reposado or añejo)
- 3 tbsps. fresh lime juice
- 2 tbsps. sugar
- 1 (3-lb) pineapple (labeled "extra sweet")

Direction

- Stir together sugar, lime juice and tequila till sugar dissolves.
- Use a large sharp knife to peel the pineapple, make sure the crown leaves are attached. Trim the bottom.
- To discard the pineapple eyes in spiral channels using a sharp paring knife: Along the row of eyes that diagonally spirals down the pineapple, cut each side to form a channel with the V shape. Discard the eyes and channel. Make the same procedure with the leftover rows of eyes.
- Preheat the oven to 425°F.
- Let the pineapple lie on its side. Carefully halve the pineapple lengthwise through the leaves, start at the base and go upward, make sure the leaves are attached. Remove the core from each half and pull out some innermost leaves that are too long to keep all of the leaves are no longer than 7 inches.
- In a 13x9-in. ceramic or glass baking dish, place the pineapple halves with the flat sides facing down. Use a skewer to pierce all the way through and all over.
- Mix the tequila mixture then place over the pineapple. Bake the pineapple with wax paper sheet layered over in the middle of the oven for 50 minutes till the pineapple caramelized lightly and tender; after every 10 minutes, baste with the juices. Cut the pineapple lengthwise in half then serve with the remaining juice in baking dish.
- You can bake the pineapple for 3 hours ahead. Use a wax paper to cover and reheat for 15-20 minutes till heated through in a 350°F.

172. Tequila And Lime Chicken Tacos

"Chicken thighs are more flavorful than chicken breast but you can use chicken breast if desired. The meat needs to be raw to absorb more flavors while cook. You can use pineapple juice, orange juice or beer instead of tequila. The liquid smoke brings a great extra kick of smoky flavor but it's optional. Serve together with refried beans, rice and a frosty glass of beer or a frozen margaritas."
Serving: Serves 6 | Prep: 5m

Ingredients

- 1 1/2 lbs. boneless, skinless chicken thighs
- 3/4 cup tequila
- 1/4 cup fresh lime juice
- 2 garlic cloves
- 2 tbsps. chopped chipotles in adobo
- 1 tbsp. chili powder
- 2 tsps. liquid smoke (optional)
- 1 tsp. ground cumin
- 1 tsp. dried oregano
- 1 tsp. ancho chile powder
- 1/2 tsp. smoked paprika
- 12 corn tortillas
- Chopped red onion
- Chopped avocado
- Chopped cilantro
- Grated quesadilla cheese
- Red salsa or pico de gallo
- 6 lime wedges

Direction

- Combine all the ingredients in the slow cooker, except the toppings and tortillas.
- Cook, covered, for 8 hours on low or for 4 hours on high.
- Place the chicken on a cutting board and use 2 forks to shred. Bring the chicken that have been shredded back to the slow cooker and stir till blended.
- In a dry skillet, warm the tortillas over medium heat and add the chicken mixture to fill. Add the toppings to serve.

173. Tequila Bloody Mary

Serving: Serves 1

Ingredients

- 1 jigger (1/2 oz.) tequila
- 1/2 cup tomato juice
- 1 tbsp. fresh lime juice
- 1/8 tsp. celery salt
- Worcestershire sauce, to taste
- Tabasco, to taste
- Garnish: 1 celery rib and 1 lime wedge

Direction

- Combine 1 1/2 cups of ice cubes with all of the ingredients in a cocktail shaker and shake well. In a tall glass, pour the mixture. Add lime wedge and celery to garnish the Bloody Mary.

174. Tequila Cooler

Serving: Serves 1

Ingredients

- 1 jigger (1 1/2 oz.) tequila
- 1 to 1 1/2 oz. Cuarenta y Tres (Spanish herbal fruit liqueur)
- Seltzer or club soda

Direction

- Stir together Cuarenta y Tres and tequila in a tall glass with 3/4 filled with ice cubes. Top off the glass with club soda or seltzer.

175. Tequila Cosmopolitan

Serving: Serves 1

Ingredients

- Lime wedge
- Sugar
- 1/4 cup blanco or reposado tequila
- 2 1/2 tbsps. thawed frozen cranberry juice concentrate
- 2 tbsps. water
- 2 tsps. fresh lime juice

Direction

- Use a lime wedge to run around a Martini glass's rim. Dip the rim into sugar. In a cocktail shaker, combine lime juice, water and cranberry juice concentrate with tequila. Add ice to fill. Shake vigorously till the drink is icy cold. Strain the drink into glass.

Nutrition Information

- Calories: 161
- Total Carbohydrate: 9 g
- Total Fat: 0 g
- Fiber: 0 g
- Protein: 0 g
- Sodium: 3 mg
- Saturated Fat: 0 g

176. Tequila Highball

"Add soda if you're in doubt. The resulting highball filled to the top with soda and 2 oz. of any booze is refreshing and can't be messed up."
Serving: 1 cocktail

Ingredients

- 1 tsp. elderflower cordial or syrup
- 1 1/2 oz. añejo tequila
- 1 lemon
- Club soda (for serving)

Direction

- In a highball glass filled with ice, stir two 3x1-in. strips lemon zest which was cut lengthwise, 1 1/2 oz. of añejo tequila and 1 tsp of elderflower syrup of cordial for 30 seconds till very cold. Add club soda to top off.
- Discard a 1-in. peel strip from a lemon with a small serrated knife; it's fine to leave some white pith. The strip should be stiff enough to be a little resistant when bent. Express oils by twisting it over the drink then remove.

Nutrition Information

- Calories: 132
- Total Carbohydrate: 10 g
- Total Fat: 0 g
- Fiber: 2 g
- Protein: 1 g
- Sodium: 2 mg
- Saturated Fat: 0 g

177. Tequila Lime Tart

Serving: Serves 6 to 8

Ingredients

- 1 1/2 cups graham cracker crumbs
- 1/4 cup unsalted butter, melted
- 1/4 cup pine nuts
- 2 tbsps. sugar
- 1 14-oz. can sweetened condensed milk
- 4 large egg yolks
- 1/2 cup fresh lime juice
- 1/4 cup tequila
- 2 egg whites
- 1 tbsp. sugar
- Whipped cream (optional)
- Fresh lime slices (optional)

Direction

- For the crust: In a processor, blend all the ingredients till it forms small clumps. On a 9-in.-diameter tart pan which has removable bottom, press the mixture onto the bottom and up the sides. You can make this 1 day ahead and keep chilled.
- For the filling: Preheat the oven to 325°F. In a medium bowl, add and stir condensed milk together with the following 3 ingredients till blended. Put aside the condensed milk mixture.
- In a large bowl, beat sugar with egg whites using an electric mixer till it forms soft peaks. Gently fold into whites with 1 1/2 cups of condensed milk mixture using a rubber spatula. Fold into whites the leftover milk mixture till just incorporated.
- Transfer the mixture into the crust. Bake for 40 minutes till there're some moist filling attached on the tester when taking it out from the center of the filling and it slightly puffs up. Place tart on a rack to cool completely. Chill for at least 2 hours and no longer than 8 hours till cold. Add lime slices and whipped cream to garnish.

Nutrition Information

- Calories: 500
- Total Carbohydrate: 62 g
- Cholesterol: 166 mg
- Total Fat: 23 g
- Fiber: 1 g
- Protein: 10 g
- Sodium: 202 mg
- Saturated Fat: 10 g

178. Tequila Mockingbird Marinade

"This marinade is nice for chicken, sea scallops and jumbo shrimp. The marinade made following the recipe is enough for 1 1/2 lbs. of poultry and seafood. You must boil any marinade coming in contact with poultry, seafood or raw meat for 1 minute before using for basting."
Serving: Makes about generous 3/4 cup

Ingredients

- 1/4 cup vegetable oil
- 3 tbsps. fresh lime juice
- 3 tbsps. tequila
- 2 tbsps. triple sec
- 1 large jalapeño chili, seeded, minced
- 1 1/2 tsps. grated lime peel
- 1 tsp. chili powder
- 1 tsp. sugar
- 1/2 tsp. coarse salt

Direction

- In a small bowl, combine all the ingredients then allow to stand for 15 minutes. You can prepare this the day before. Store in the fridge, covered.
- Marinate seafood for 30 minutes and poultry for 1-3 hours in the fridge. Don't pat dry but drain and grill. In a heavy small saucepan, bring the leftover marinade to a boil for 1 minute. Sprinkle over seafood or poultry with some of the marinade before serving.

Nutrition Information

- Calories: 182
- Total Carbohydrate: 6 g
- Total Fat: 14 g
- Fiber: 0 g
- Protein: 0 g
- Sodium: 117 mg
- Saturated Fat: 1 g

179. Tequila Mojito

Serving: Serves 1

Ingredients

- 3 tbsps. fresh lime juice
- 4 tsps. sugar
- 12 large fresh mint leaves
- 1/4 cup blanco or reposado tequila
- 1/4 cup club soda

Direction

- Mix mint, sugar and lime juice in a highball glass. Use a spoon's back to mash the mint leaves till the sugar is dissolved. Add ice to fill the glass. Stir in club soda and tequila till blended.

Nutrition Information

- Calories: 205
- Total Carbohydrate: 21 g
- Total Fat: 0 g
- Fiber: 0 g
- Protein: 0 g
- Sodium: 15 mg
- Saturated Fat: 0 g

180. Tequila Shrimp

"An excellent and simple recipe to serve over pasta."
Serving: 6 | Prep: 10m | Ready in: 20m

Ingredients

- 2 tbsps. unsalted butter
- 4 cloves garlic, chopped
- 1 1/2 lbs. large shrimp - peeled and deveined
- 1/2 cup tequila
- 1/2 cup chopped fresh cilantro
- salt and pepper to taste

Direction

- In a big skillet, melt butter over medium heat. Sauté garlic till light brown. Place and cook shrimp in the pan for 3 minutes.
- Add in tequila and season with pepper, salt and cilantro. Cook for 2 minutes longer.

Nutrition Information

- Calories: 205 calories;
- Total Carbohydrate: 1.7 g
- Cholesterol: 157 mg
- Total Fat: 7.9 g
- Protein: 19.8 g
- Sodium: 174 mg

181. Tequila Sour

Serving: Serves 1.

Ingredients

- 2-3 oz. tequila
- 2 tbsps. lemon juice
- 1/2-1 tsp. superfine sugar
- 3 or 4 ice cubes
- 1 orange or lemon slice or peel
- Maraschino cherry

Direction

- In a cocktail shaker, combine all the ingredients, except the cherry and fruit slice or peel. Shake vigorously then strain the drink into a Delmonico or a sour glass. Add cherry and fruit for garnish. You can use 1 6-oz. wine glass instead of the traditional sour glass.

182. Tequila Sunrise

"This hot-day drink is pretty with layers of grenadine and orange juice. The high ratio of juice to tequila can make it a great choice to serve at a brunch cocktail."
Serving: 1 | Prep: 5m | Ready in: 5m

Ingredients

- 1 (1.5 fluid oz.) jigger tequila
- 3/4 cup freshly squeezed orange juice
- ice cubes
- 1/2 (1.5 fluid oz.) jigger grenadine syrup
- 1 slice orange, for garnish
- 1 maraschino cherry for garnish

Direction

- Shake or stir orange juice and tequila together. Add ice cubes to fill a chilled 12-oz. glass. Place in the orange juice mixture. Pour the grenadine in gradually; be patient and let it settle to the glass's bottom. Add a maraschino cherry and a slice of orange as garnish.

183. Tequila Sunrise Cocktail

"This cocktail has a two-toned and sunrise-like appearance."
Serving: 1 | Prep: 5m | Ready in: 5m

Ingredients

- 1 1/2 cups ice
- 2 fluid oz. tequila
- 4 fluid oz. orange juice
- 1 cup ice
- 3/4 fluid oz. grenadine syrup

Direction

- Add 1 1/2 cups of ice to fill a highball glass and put aside.
- In a cocktail mixing glass, combine orange juice and tequila. Stir in 1 cup of ice and strain the drink into the prepped highball glass.

Gradually add in grenadine then allow to settle.
- Stir then drink.

Nutrition Information

- Calories: 263 calories;
- Total Carbohydrate: 31.8 g
- Cholesterol: 0 mg
- Total Fat: 0.2 g
- Protein: 0.9 g
- Sodium: 27 mg

184. Tequila Sunrise II

Serving: Serves 1

Ingredients

- Cracked ice
- 1/2 cup orange juice
- 2 ponies (2 oz.) tequila
- Lime juice, to taste
- 1 tsp. grenadine
- Garnish: slice of lime

Direction

- Fill cracked ice in half of a 12-oz. glass. Stir in lime juice, tequila and orange juice. Sprinkle grenadine, don't stir, on the drink. Add a slice of lime as garnish.

185. Tequila Tamarindo

"A fizzy cocktail for the summer."
Serving: Makes 6

Ingredients

- 8 oz. tamarind paste (from seedless pliable block), coarsely chopped (about 1 cup)
- 5 cups water, divided
- 1 4-oz. piece fresh ginger, peeled, thinly sliced into rounds (scant 1 cup)
- 1 cup sugar

- 12 orange slices, divided
- 3/4 cup silver (or white) tequila
- 1/4 cup fresh lime juice
- 1/4 tsp. coarse kosher salt
- Ice cubes
- 3 cups chilled club soda, divided

Direction

- Boil 2 cups of water and tamarind in a small saucepan. Lower the heat and simmer for 25 minutes while using a wooden spoon to breaking up and stirring often till soft. Put on a strainer placed over bowl. Extract puree of the tamarind by pressing on it. Remove solids in the strainer. Let cool.
- In a separate small saucepan, boil sugar, ginger and 1 cup of water while stirring till sugar is dissolved. Lower the heat and let simmer for 20 minutes. Let the ginger syrup cool.
- Place in a large pitcher's bottom with 6 orange slices. Use the handle of a wooden spoon or use a muddler to mash. In the same pitcher, strain the ginger syrup and remove the ginger. Stir in 2 cups of water, salt, lime juice, tequila and 1 cup of tamarind puree till blended. Let chill till cold.
- Add ice to fill 6 tall glasses. Pour the tamarind drink into glasses. Add 1/2 cup of chilled club soda on top of each glass and place 1 orange slice to garnish each drink.

186. Tequila, Apple, And Dried Cranberry Compote

Serving: Makes 10 servings

Ingredients

- 3 lbs. Granny Smith apples (about 8 medium), peeled, cored, cut into 1/2-inch pieces
- 2 1/4 cups apple cider
- 1 3/4 cups dried cranberries
- 3/4 cup tequila
- 1/2 cup sugar
- 1 cinnamon stick
- 3/4 tsp. ground black pepper

Direction

- In a large pot, combine all of the ingredients. Bring the pot of the mixture to simmer over medium heat. Cook for 20 minutes while stirring occasionally till cranberries are plump and apples are tender. Let the mixture cool to room temperature. Store in the fridge, covered, for 2 hours to well chill the compote. You can prepare the compote up to one day ahead then store in the fridge.

Nutrition Information

- Calories: 248
- Total Carbohydrate: 53 g
- Total Fat: 1 g
- Fiber: 5 g
- Protein: 1 g
- Sodium: 5 mg
- Saturated Fat: 0 g

187. Tequila-lime Mahi Mahi Tacos

"The flavors of our zesty marinade is taken on by the mild mahi mahi."
Serving: Makes 4 servings

Ingredients

- 4 tbsps. fresh lime juice, divided
- 3 tbsps. tequila
- 3 tbsps. roughly chopped fresh cilantro, divided
- 1 tsp. finely chopped garlic
- 1 tsp. ground cumin
- 1 lb mahimahi
- 3 tbsps. rice wine vinegar
- 1 tsp. canola oil
- 2 3/4 tsps. honey, divided
- 1 1/2 tsps. kosher salt, divided
- 1/2 tsp. freshly ground black pepper, divided
- 3 cups thinly sliced red cabbage

- 3/4 cup reduced-fat sour cream
- 3 tbsps. 2 percent milk
- 1 1/2 tsps. finely grated lime zest
- 8 corn tortillas (6 inches each)
- 1/2 firm-ripe avocado, thinly sliced
- 2 limes, quartered

Direction

- Combine cumin, garlic, 1 tbsp. of cilantro, tequila and 3 tbsp. of lime juice in a resealable plastic bag. Place in fish, seal the bag then turn till coated. Store in the fridge for 1 hour, turning one time. Combine 1/4 tsp of pepper, 1/4 tsp of salt, 2 tsp of honey, oil and vinegar in a bowl. Place in cabbage and toss well. Add 1/2 tsp of salt, the leftover 3/4 tsp of honey, the leftover 1 tbsp. of juice, zest, milk and sour cream in a separate bowl. Heat the grill. Take the fish from the marinade then add the leftover 1/4 tsp of pepper and the leftover 1/2 tsp of salt to season. Grill for 4 minutes each side till it's lightly charred and just cooked through, turning one time. Place on a cutting board and chop coarsely. Add the leftover 2 tbsp. of cilantro in the slaw and stir. Grill tortillas for 30 seconds each side, turning one time. Place in each tortilla's center with 1 tbsp. of sour cream mixture to assemble. Place avocado, slaw and fish onto tortillas. Add lime wedges for garnish.

Nutrition Information

- Calories: 412
- Total Carbohydrate: 42 g
- Cholesterol: 99 mg
- Total Fat: 14 g
- Fiber: 7 g
- Protein: 29 g
- Sodium: 886 mg
- Saturated Fat: 5 g

188. Tequini

"The almighty martini is added a Latin twist from tequila."
Serving: 1 | Prep: 4m | Ready in: 4m

Ingredients

- 2 (1.5 fluid oz.) jiggers tequila
- 1/2 fluid oz. dry vermouth
- 1/2 fluid oz. orange bitters
- 1 twist lemon zest, garnish

Direction

- Combine orange bitters, vermouth and tequila in an ice-filled cocktail shaker. Shake well then strain the drink into a cocktail glass. Add a twist of lime for garnish.

189. Texas Tea I

"Double the tequila and omit the gin and this makes the same thing as a Long Island Iced Tea."
Serving: 1 | Prep: 3m | Ready in: 3m

Ingredients

- 1/2 fluid oz. vodka
- 1/2 fluid oz. rum
- 1 fluid oz. tequila
- 1/2 lemon, juiced
- 1 tbsp. cola-flavored carbonated beverage

Direction

- Mix cola, lemon juice, tequila, rum, and vodka together in a cocktail mixer. Stir the mixture. Put it into a glass with a lot of ice.

190. Texas Tea III

"The standard Bartender's recipe for a Texas Tea with the tequila."
Serving: 1 | Prep: 1m | Ready in: 1m

Ingredients

- 1/2 fluid oz. vodka
- 1/2 fluid oz. amber rum
- 1/2 fluid oz. gold tequila
- 1/2 fluid oz. triple sec liqueur
- 1/4 cup sweet-and-sour cocktail mix
- 1/4 cup cola-flavored carbonated beverage
- 1 wedge lemon
- 1 wedge lime

Direction

- Combine triple sec, tequila, rum and vodka in an ice-filled tall glass. Place cola and equal parts of sweet-and-sour on top. Squeeze over the top with lime wedge and lemon wedge. Stir.

191. Texatini

"Another great way to serve margarita! Keep in mind this drink is a bit strong."
Serving: 1 | Prep: 15m | Ready in: 15m

Ingredients

- coarse salt (optional)
- 1 (1.5 fluid oz.) jigger tequila
- 1 (1.5 fluid oz.) jigger orange liqueur (Cointreau, Triple Sec or Grand Marnier)
- 1/2 cup sweet and sour mix
- 1 fluid oz. orange juice
- 1 cup crushed ice
- 1 jalapeno-stuffed green olive

Direction

- Dampen the rim of a large martini glass a little bit then dip it in coarse salt to coat the rim.

- In a shaker, put in the sweet and sour mix, tequila, ice, orange liqueur and orange juice. Shake vigorously to mix everything together then strain the mixture directly into the prepared martini glass. Serve it with jalapeño-stuffed green olives for presentation.

192. The Best Margarita Mix !!!

"This recipe is inspired by the margaritas that we enjoyed drinking at the old port of Montreal."
Serving: 4 | Prep: 10m | Ready in: 10m

Ingredients

- 1/2 cup tequila
- 1/2 cup triple sec
- 1/4 cup freshly squeezed lime juice
- 2 tbsps. honey
- 4 cups ice

Direction

- Blend the ice, triple sec, lime juice, tequila, and honey in a blender until smooth.

Nutrition Information

- Calories: 214 calories;
- Total Carbohydrate: 24 g
- Cholesterol: 0 mg
- Total Fat: 0.1 g
- Protein: 0.1 g
- Sodium: 11 mg

193. The Best Raspberry Margarita!

"It's a delectable raspberry-seasoned margarita recipe that is inspired by one of the huge chains that's popular for its margaritas! Make sure to utilize top-quality tequila and raspberry alcohol for more extreme impact. I, in some cases, like to include a 'floater' of Chambord to finish everything off."

Serving: 1 | Prep: 5m | Ready in: 5m

Ingredients

- 5 fluid oz. sweet-and-sour cocktail mix
- 2 fluid oz. premium tequila
- 1 fluid oz. cointreau
- 1 fluid oz. Chambord (raspberry liqueur)
- 2 cups ice cubes
- margarita salt
- 1 lime, cut into 4 wedges

Direction

- Combine raspberry liqueur, tequila, sweet and sour mix, and Cointreau in a shaker filled with ice. Shake until the shaker is cold on the outside.
- Rub the lime wedge around the rim of the margarita glass and dip it into the salt. Add a few ice cubes into the margarita glass then strain liquid from the shaker carefully. Before serving, garnish the glass with a lime wedge.

194. The Classic Margarita

"A classic recipe that demands good spirits."
Serving: Makes 1 drink

Ingredients

- 2 oz. tequila made from 100 percent agave, preferably reposado or blanco
- 1 oz. Cointreau
- 1 oz. freshly squeezed lime juice
- Salt for garnish

Direction

- In an ice-filled cocktail shaker, combine lime juice, Cointreau and tequila. Use water or lime juice to moisten rim of Margarita or any other cocktail glass. Keep the glass upside down to dip rim into the salt. Shake then strain into glass to serve.

Nutrition Information

- Calories: 203
- Total Carbohydrate: 2 g
- Total Fat: 0 g
- Fiber: 0 g
- Protein: 0 g
- Sodium: 1 mg
- Saturated Fat: 0 g

195. The Daytona Destroyer

"An excellent cocktail recipe you should whip up on race day!"
Serving: 4 | Prep: 15m | Ready in: 15m

Ingredients

- 2 (1/4-inch thick) cucumber slices
- 1 oz. agave nectar
- 1 thinly sliced serrano chile
- 6 oz. tequila
- 4 oz. club soda
- 3 oz. freshly squeezed lime juice
- 4 cucumber slices for garnishes

Direction

- In a beaker, muddle sliced chile, agave nectar and cucumber. Add a few big ice cubes, lime juice, club soda and tequila. Vigorously stir.
- Put crushed ice into four cocktail glasses.
- Into prepped glasses, strain mixture. Top with a cucumber slice.

Nutrition Information

- Calories: 130 calories;
- Total Carbohydrate: 8.7 g

- Cholesterol: 0 mg
- Total Fat: 0.1 g
- Protein: 0.3 g
- Sodium: 2 mg

196. The Perfect Blended Margarita

"You can serve this pre-made margarita mix straight-up or add salt to the rim if desired."
Serving: 4 | Prep: 10m | Ready in: 10m

Ingredients

- 1 1/4 cups fresh lime juice
- 1 cup Triple Sec or other orange liqueur
- 1 cup silver tequila
- 3 tbsps. fresh lemon juice
- 3 cups ice cubes

Direction

- In a blender, combine 2 cups of ice, lemon juice, tequila, triple sec and lime juice then blend till smooth.
- In a cocktail shaker, add 1 cup of ice cubes and the preferred amount of margarita. Cover then shake well to serve.

197. The Real Long Island Iced Tea

"The best Long Island Iced Teas ever!""
Serving: 1 | Prep: 10m | Ready in: 10m

Ingredients

- 1/2 fluid oz. vodka
- 1/2 fluid oz. rum
- 1/2 fluid oz. gin
- 1/2 fluid oz. tequila
- 1/2 fluid oz. triple sec (orange-flavored liqueur)
- 1 fluid oz. sweet and sour mix
- 1 fluid oz. cola, or to taste
- 1 lemon slice

Direction

- Fill ice into a cocktail shaker. Pour in vodka, sour mix, gin, triple sec, tequila, and rum mix over ice; take a cover and shake. Pour cocktail into a hurricane glass or Collins glass; place splash of cola for color on the top. Garnish a lemon slice.

Nutrition Information

- Calories: 262 calories;
- Total Carbohydrate: 23.3 g
- Cholesterol: 0 mg
- Total Fat: 0.1 g
- Protein: 0.2 g
- Sodium: 3 mg

198. The Ultimate Margarita

"Make the best margarita with the best ingredients."
Serving: 1

Ingredients

- 1/2 fluid oz. Gran Gala Triple Orange Liqueur
- 2 fluid oz. Corazon Blanco Tequila
- 1 fluid oz. fresh lime juice
- 1 fluid oz. agave nectar or simple syrup

Direction

- Shake all the ingredients together with ice; filter into a margarita glass.
- If preferred, moisten the rim of the glass with a slice of lime then dab in salt. Garnish with a wedge of lime on the rim of the glass.

Nutrition Information

- Calories: 274 calories;
- Total Carbohydrate: 31.6 g
- Cholesterol: 0 mg
- Total Fat: 0.1 g
- Protein: 0.1 g
- Sodium: 2 mg

199. Tiki Cantaloupe-coconut Cocktail

"The combination of coconut and fresh cantaloupe will make 1 perfect summer cocktail."
Serving: Serves 4

Ingredients

- 1 medium cantaloupe
- 1/2 cup unsweetened coconut milk
- 1/2 cup tequila
- 1/4 cup Midori or tequila
- 1/4 cup fresh lime juice
- 1/4 cup agave nectar
- Mint sprigs and lime wheels (for serving)

Direction

- Cut off the rind from both cantaloupe's ends in a thin piece. Halve crosswise and discard seeds. Scoop the flesh out and put the cantaloupe halves aside.
- Place 1/2 of the flesh in a blender and save up the remaining for use later. Add 1/2 cup of ice, agave nectar, lime juice, Midori, tequila and coconut milk then blend till smooth.
- Pour the cocktail into the melon halves that have been reserved and fill with ice. Add lime wheels and mint sprigs to garnish. Place 2 straws in each to serve.

200. Top Shelf Margaritas On The Rocks

""Fresh ingredients bring to a quality result with the avid 'rita fanatic""
Serving: 16 | Prep: 10m | Ready in: 10m

Ingredients

- 2/3 cup sugar
- 1/3 cup water
- 2 1/4 cups water
- 1 1/2 cups fresh lemon juice
- 1/4 cup sugar
- 1 egg white
- 2 cups ice cubes
- 2 cups premium tequila
- 1 cup Cointreau
- 1/2 cup lime juice
- 16 lime wedges
- coarse kosher salt

Direction

- To make a simple syrup: stir together 1/3 cup water and 2/3 cup sugar, bringing to a boil until the sugar dissolves; take aside to rest.
- To make the sour mix: briskly stir together the lemon juice, 2 1/4 cups water, egg white, and 1/4 cup sugar; take aside.
- In a pitcher, mix the ice cubes, 1/2 cup of the sour mix, Cointreau, tequila, 1 oz. of the simple syrup, and lime juice; stir vigorously in 8 to 15 seconds to infuse the ice.
- Run along the rim of an 8-oz. glass with a lime wedge. On a plate, drizzle the kosher salt and coat by dipping the glass rims in the salt; if desired, add ice. Pour the mixture from the cocktail shaker into the glass. Serve.

201. Top Shelf Sparkling Margarita Jell-o®

"A flavorful, salty, tart, and sweet imitation of cold margarita for adults. Add lime wedge on top to serve."
Serving: 24 | Prep: 15m | Ready in: 4h30m

Ingredients

- 3 (3 oz.) packages lime-flavored gelatin mix (such as Jell-O®)
- 1 (3 oz.) package lemon-flavored gelatin mix (such as Jell-O®)
- 2 1/2 cups boiling water
- 1 2/3 cups premium tequila
- 2/3 cup triple sec
- 2/3 cup brandy-based orange liqueur (such as Grand Marnier®)
- 1/2 cup sweetened lime juice
- 2 cups sparkling water

- 1 lime, zested
- 1 pinch margarita salt, or as needed

Direction

- In a bowl with boiling water, mix in lemon gelatin and lime gelatin until completely dissolved. Refrigerate to chill for 15 minutes.
- Combine the gelatin mixture, tequila, sweetened lime juice, orange liqueur, and triple sec; softly mix in sparkling water. Transfer mixture in twenty-four small cups; add lime zest in each cup. Place in the refrigerator for 4 hours until set. Sprinkle margarita salt in each cup then serve.

Nutrition Information

- Calories: 144 calories;
- Total Carbohydrate: 20 g
- Cholesterol: 0 mg
- Total Fat: 0 g
- Protein: 1.3 g
- Sodium: 69 mg

202. Top-shelf Margaritas

Serving: Makes 4 servings

Ingredients

- 1 lime wedge for coating rims of glasses
- Kosher salt for coating rims of glasses
- 2 cups ice cubes
- 3/4 cup Grand Marnier
- 3/4 cup premium, aged, añejo tequila
- 1/2 cup fresh lime juice
- Garnish: 4 lime wedges

Direction

- Use lime wedge to rub on the rims of 4 stemmed glasses. Lightly coat the rims by dipping them in salt. Combine the leftover ingredients in a cocktail shaker then shake well. In the glasses, strain the drink and add lime wedges to garnish.

Nutrition Information

- Calories: 201
- Total Carbohydrate: 3 g
- Total Fat: 0 g
- Fiber: 0 g
- Protein: 0 g
- Sodium: 545 mg
- Saturated Fat: 0 g

203. Toreador

Serving: Serves 1.

Ingredients

- 2 oz. tequila
- 1 oz. dark crème de cacao
- 1 oz. heavy cream
- 1/4 tsp. unsweetened cocoa powder
- 3 or 4 ice cubes

Direction

- Combine ice cubes, cream, crème de cacao and tequila in a cocktail shaker then shake vigorously. Into a cocktail glass, strain and add cocoa as garnish.

204. Trieste Tequila Cooler

"Garnish this tequila and Gran Gala cooler with an orange, lime juice and fresh cilantro to have a perfect cocktail for warm-weather days."
Serving: 1

Ingredients

- 1 fluid oz. Gran Gala Triple Orange Liqueur
- 2 fluid oz. Corazon Blanco Tequila
- 1/2 fluid oz. lime juice
- 1 1/2 tbsps. fresh cilantro
- San Pellegrino sparking mineral water
- 1 slice orange

Direction

- Muddle 1.5 tbsp. of fresh cilantro with lime juice.
- Stir in Gran Gala Orange Liqueur and Blanco Tequila with ice. In a glass filled with ice, strain the drink and place Pellegrino on top.
- Add orange to garnish.

Nutrition Information

- Calories: 241 calories;
- Total Carbohydrate: 15.4 g
- Cholesterol: 0 mg
- Total Fat: 0.1 g
- Protein: 0.3 g
- Sodium: 7 mg

205. Tropical Margarita

Serving: Makes 2 drinks

Ingredients

- 9 tbsps. frozen guava-passion-orange concentrate, thawed
- 1/2 cup tequila
- 4 tsps. frozen limeade, thawed
- 4 tsps. fresh lime juice
- 16 ice cubes, coarsely cracked
- Optional garnishes: Fresh lime slices
- Orange-peel twists

Direction

- In a glass measuring cup, combine the initial 4 ingredients. Add ice to fill 2 Margarita glasses. Pour over with the Margarita mixture. Add orange peel twists and lime slices as garnish, if preferred.

206. Turquoise Margarita

"This refreshing cocktail features fresh lime peel and blue curacao."
Serving: 6 servings

Ingredients

- 6 lime slices
- Coarse salt
- 1 1/4 cups Margarita mix
- 3/4 cup tequila
- 1/4 cup blue curaçao
- 1/2 lime, quartered
- 4 cups ice

Direction

- Moisten the rim of each six stemmed glasses with slices of lime; keep the lime slices. Dab rims of glasses in salt. In a blender, process Margarita mix and the following three ingredients together. Process until the lime is finely minced; add ice. Continue blending until the mixture is smooth and thick. Transfer to glasses and add slices of lime as garnish.

207. Twisted Stripper

"A smooth mixed drink with many different ingredients."
Serving: 1 | Prep: 5m | Ready in: 5m

Ingredients

- 1/2 fluid oz. Canadian whiskey
- 1/2 fluid oz. tequila
- 1/2 fluid oz. 151 proof rum
- 1/2 fluid oz. vodka
- 1/2 fluid oz. raspberry flavored liqueur
- 1/2 fluid oz. coconut-flavored rum
- 1/2 fluid oz. triple sec
- 1 fluid oz. sweet and sour mix
- 1 fluid oz. lemon-lime soda
- 1 fluid oz. pineapple juice
- 1 cup ice cubes

- 1 dash grenadine syrup

Direction

- In a cocktail shaker, combine ice, pineapple juice, lemon-lime soda, sour and sweet mix, triple sec, coconut rum, raspberry liqueur, vodka, 151 proof rum, tequila and whisky. Shake then strain into an ice-filled glass. Add a dash of grenadine syrup on top.

208. Ultimate Frozen Strawberry Jalapeno Margarita

"Here's another variation of an ultimate frozen strawberry margarita. Best when served in a margarita glass with its rim dipped in a coarse salt or powdered sugar."
Serving: 4 | Prep: 10m | Ready in: 10m

Ingredients

- 4 cups ice, or as needed
- 6 fluid oz. tequila
- 2 fluid oz. elderflower liqueur (such as St. Germain®)
- 4 slices jalapeno pepper, or to taste
- 8 oz. frozen sweetened strawberries, thawed
- 3 fluid oz. frozen limeade concentrate
- 1 fluid oz. frozen strawberry daiquiri concentrate

Direction

- Put the ice in a blender. Blend the ice until it is crushed. Pour in jalapeno pepper slices, tequila, and elderflower liqueur. Add the strawberry daiquiri concentrate, limeade, and strawberries into the mixture. Blend it for 30 seconds until smooth.

Nutrition Information

- Calories: 289 calories;
- Total Carbohydrate: 42.6 g
- Cholesterol: 0 mg
- Total Fat: 0.1 g
- Protein: 0.4 g

- Sodium: 11 mg

209. Ultimate Frozen Strawberry Margarita

"Strawberry margarita with frozen strawberries and limeade concentrate. Why not?"
Serving: 4 | Prep: 5m | Ready in: 5m

Ingredients

- 6 fluid oz. tequila
- 2 fluid oz. triple sec
- 8 oz. frozen sliced strawberries in syrup
- 4 fluid oz. frozen limeade concentrate

Direction

- Fill ice and crush into a blender. Add in the triple sec and tequila. Add the limeade and strawberries, to blend until smooth, about 30 seconds. Dip the rims in powdered sugar. Serve into margarita glasses.

210. Vampiros Mexicanos (mexican Vampires)

"A recipe for a real Mexican cocktail. One glass of this drink include the best of Mexico: sangrita – the favorite tequila chaser of the Mexican and tequila."
Serving: 1 | Prep: 5m | Ready in: 5m

Ingredients

- ice cubes, or as needed
- 1 1/2 fluid oz. silver tequila (100% agave)
- 3 oz. sangrita (Mexican-style bloody mary mix with orange and lime)
- 1 1/2 oz. citrus-flavored soda (such as Squirt®)
- 1/2 lime, juiced
- 1 pinch Mexican-style chili powder with lime (such as Tajin® fruit seasoning)

Direction

- Add ice cubes to fill a highball glass. Stir in fruit seasoning powder, lime juice, citrus soda, sangrita and tequila till mixed well.

Nutrition Information

- Calories: 143 calories;
- Total Carbohydrate: 10.6 g
- Cholesterol: 0 mg
- Total Fat: 0.2 g
- Protein: 1 g
- Sodium: 432 mg

211. Watermelon And Strawberry Margarita

"You won't need for ice if you freeze the strawberries and watermelon before making the drink. Freezing also help retain the full intensity of the fruit flavors."
Serving: Makes 4 Servings

Ingredients

- 3 cups (packed) frozen chopped seeded watermelon
- 1 cup (packed) frozen quartered unsweetened strawberries
- 7 tbsps. tequila
- 7 tbsps. triple sec
- 1/3 cup fresh lime juice
- 2 tbsps. sugar
- Pinch of salt
- 4 small thin watermelon wedges

Direction

- In a blender, puree the initial 7 ingredients till smooth. In chilled margarita glasses, pour the drink and add watermelon wedges for garnish.

Nutrition Information

- Calories: 251
- Total Carbohydrate: 38 g

- Total Fat: 1 g
- Fiber: 2 g
- Protein: 2 g
- Sodium: 78 mg
- Saturated Fat: 0 g

212. Watermelon Margarita Ice Pops

Serving: Makes 8 ice pops | Prep: 15m

Ingredients

- 5 cups chopped seedless watermelon (1 1/4 lbs.)
- 2 tbsps. fresh lime juice
- 3 tbsps. superfine granulated sugar
- 1/4 cup water
- 1/4 cup silver tequila
- Equipment: 8 (1/3-cup) ice pop molds and 8 wooden sticks
- 0 and 8 wooden sticks

Direction

- In a blender, purée all the ingredients till smooth. With a fine-mesh sieve, strain the mixture into a big measuring cup, press on then remove the solids. Skim off the foam and transfer into molds. Store in the freezer for 30 minutes. Place sticks in then freeze for 24 hours till firm.

213. Watermelon Margaritas

"A fantastic drink for the summer season!"
Serving: 4 | Prep: 10m | Ready in: 10m

Ingredients

- 2 cups cubed seeded watermelon
- 2 cups crushed ice
- 1/3 cup tequila
- 1/4 cup white sugar
- 1/4 cup lime juice

- 1 tbsp. vodka
- 1 tbsp. orange liqueur

Direction

- Use a blender to thoroughly mix the tequila, vodka, watermelon, orange liqueur, sugar, lime juice and ice together. Put the margarita mixture into individual glasses.

Nutrition Information

- Calories: 139 calories;
- Total Carbohydrate: 21.1 g
- Cholesterol: 0 mg
- Total Fat: 0.1 g
- Protein: 0.5 g
- Sodium: 3 mg

214. Watermelon Refresher

""This recipe is surprisingly refreshing and simple! You can use the blender piece as your pitcher if you wanted to.""
Serving: 10 | Prep: 10m | Ready in: 10m

Ingredients

- 10 cups diced seeded watermelon
- 1/2 cup water
- 1/3 cup agave nectar
- 1 1/2 cups tequila (such as Patron®)
- 1 cup frozen blueberries
- 1 sprig mint leaves, for garnish

Direction

- In a blender, blend the watermelon until it's smooth. Pour the blended watermelon into a large pitcher.
- In a small bowl, mix the agave nectar and water and pour the mixture into the watermelon. Mix the tequila into the watermelon mixture. Before serving, add some blueberries and garnish it with a mint.

Nutrition Information

- Calories: 164 calories;
- Total Carbohydrate: 21.9 g
- Cholesterol: 0 mg
- Total Fat: 0.3 g
- Protein: 1 g
- Sodium: 2 mg

215. Watermelon, Lime, And Tequila

"A perfect slushy blender cocktail to while away the summer hours."
Serving: 4 servings

Ingredients

- 3 1/2 cups watermelon pieces, frozen
- 1/2"-thick jalapeño slice, with seeds
- 6 oz. tequila blanco
- 4 oz. simple syrup
- 2 oz. fresh lime juice
- 3 cups ice
- Optional garnish: Watermelon wedges and sliced jalapeños

Direction

- Combine 3 cups of ice, 2 oz. of fresh lime juice, 4 oz. of simple syrup, 6 oz. of tequila blanco, 1/2-in.-thick jalapeño slice, with seeds and 3 1/2 cups frozen watermelon pieces. Garnish with sliced jalapeños and watermelon wedges if desired.
- Peak-season fruit can be found at farmers' market. Place a single layer of the fruit on a baking sheet lined with parchment paper then freeze till solid. In a blender, purée till very thick and smooth. Transfer into glasses to serve.
- It's better when the ice is dry. For a watery cocktail, melt the ice.
- The old blender is good enough to do the trick finely so there's no need to upgrade to a new one.

- When you pour the drinks into glass, they should look too thick but they'll immediately loosen.

Nutrition Information

- Calories: 219
- Total Carbohydrate: 32 g
- Total Fat: 0 g
- Fiber: 1 g
- Protein: 1 g
- Sodium: 26 mg
- Saturated Fat: 0 g

216. Watermelon-cucumber Margarita

Serving: Makes 2 drinks

Ingredients

- 1 1/2 cups 1-inch chunks rindless watermelon
- 6 (1/8-inch-thick) slices English hothouse cucumber
- 15 large fresh mint leaves
- 1/2 cup 100% blue agave silver tequila
- 1/4 cup fresh lime juice
- 3 tbsps. Simple Syrup
- 1 tbsp. Cointreau or other orange liqueur
- 2 cups ice cubes, divided
- 2 small watermelon triangles, each skewered with 1 cucumber round (for garnish)
- 2 fresh mint sprigs (for garnish)

Direction

- In a medium-sized bowl, put in the first 3 ingredients. Use a muddler or the back of a wooden spoon to mash the solids firmly until the mixture is well-crushed. Add in the simple syrup, tequila, Cointreau, lime juice and 1 cup of ice then mix everything until well-combined. Strain the mixture directly into a large glass measuring cup. Distribute the remaining ice evenly among 2 tall glasses. Fill each glass with the margarita mixture. Serve it with mint sprigs and watermelon skewers for a nice presentation.

Nutrition Information

- Calories: 280
- Total Carbohydrate: 35 g
- Total Fat: 0 g
- Fiber: 1 g
- Protein: 1 g
- Sodium: 17 mg
- Saturated Fat: 0 g

217. Wonderful Margarita

"You can add salt to the glass rim of this delicious and refreshing classic margarita if desired."
Serving: 6 | Prep: 10m | Ready in: 10m

Ingredients

- 8 cups ice
- 6 fluid oz. tequila
- 4 fluid oz. frozen limeade concentrate
- 4 fluid oz. lime margarita mix
- 2 fluid oz. frozen orange juice concentrate
- 1 fluid oz. triple sec
- 1 lime, sliced into wedges (optional)

Direction

- In a blender, blend triple sec, orange juice concentrate, margarita mix, limeade concentrate, tequila and ice till smooth.
- Transfer margaritas into glasses and add a lime slice to garnish.

Nutrition Information

- Calories: 180 calories;
- Total Carbohydrate: 26.4 g
- Cholesterol: 0 mg
- Total Fat: 0 g
- Protein: 0.3 g
- Sodium: 24 mg

218. Wonderful Margaritas

""It's so simple to prepare. Whenever I presented this to anyone, they would always ask for more.""
Serving: 12 | Prep: 15m | Ready in: 15m

Ingredients

- 2 (12 fluid oz.) cans frozen limeade concentrate
- 1 liter artificially sweetened citrus soda
- 12 fluid oz. tequila

Direction

- Empty the limeade into a 2-quart pitcher. Fill each of the empty limeade cans twice with citrus soda and pour it into the pitcher. Pour tequila in one of the limeade cans and stir it into the pitcher. You can adjust the alcohol according to your taste. Stir well; serve.

219. Yucatan Margarita With Tropical Fruit

"This Margarita is served at a restaurant and made with cream of coconut and guava and papaya nectars."
Serving: 12 Servings

Ingredients

- Lime wedges
- Sugar
- 3 cups Homemade Sweet-and-Sour Mix for Margaritas
- 1 cup gold tequila
- 12 tbsps. papaya nectar
- 12 tbsps. guava nectar
- 1/2 cup canned cream of coconut available in the liquor department of most supermarkets.
- 16 ice cubes
- 12 lime slices

Direction

- Use lime wedges to brush rims of twelve glasses. Then dip the rims in sugar.
- In a blender, mix 1/4 cup cream of coconut, 1 1/2 cups sweet-and-sour mix, 6 tbsps. guava nectar, 1/2 cup tequila, 8 ice cubes, and 6 tbsps. papaya nectar. Then process until combined. Transfer into six glasses. Repeat this with the remaining cream of coconut, sweet-and-sour mix, both nectars, ice cubes and tequila. Transfer into six glasses. Decorate each with lime slice.

220. Yummy Margaritas

"This is a recipe for a frozen margarita that is made with beer."
Serving: 2 | Prep: 5m | Ready in: 5m

Ingredients

- 1 (12 fluid oz.) can frozen limeade concentrate
- 6 fluid oz. beer
- 6 fluid oz. tequila
- 4 cups ice
- 1 lime, sliced

Direction

- Combine tequila, beer, and limeade in a blender. Fill the blender with ice up to its top. Blend the mixture until smooth and thick.
- Surround the rims of the 2 large margarita glasses with salt. You can do it by putting salt into the small plate. Use a damp towel to moisten the rims of the glasses. Press the rims into the salt.
- Pour the margarita into the salted glasses. Garnish the drink with slices of lime.

Index

A

Ale, 40, 66

Almond, 33

Apple, 5, 17, 52, 60, 77

Avocado, 3–4, 24, 49–50, 67, 72, 78

B

Baking, 29–30, 48, 66, 71, 87

Banana, 3–4, 11, 19, 24, 69

Basil, 4, 18, 22, 69

Beans, 72

Beef, 4, 66

Beer, 3–4, 10–12, 16, 20–21, 32, 39, 44, 48–50, 63–64, 69–70, 72, 89

Berry, 4, 41, 66, 70

Black pepper, 65, 77

Blackberry, 3, 12–13

Blueberry, 22, 41, 87

Brandy, 8, 21, 26, 28, 44, 47, 51, 60, 62, 82

Broth, 67

Butter, 27, 31, 43, 73, 75

C

Cabbage, 77–78

Cake, 3, 31–32, 43

Cayenne pepper, 25

Celery, 3, 6, 22, 72

Champagne, 51

Cheese, 43, 65–66, 72

Cherry, 15, 17, 28, 59, 75–76

Chicken, 5, 67, 72, 74

Chicken breast, 72

Chicken thigh, 72

Chipotle, 3, 17, 50, 64, 72

Cider, 3, 17–18, 52, 77

Cinnamon, 4, 31–33, 51, 53, 57, 77

Citrus fruit, 22

Cloves, 49, 72, 75

Cocktail, 3–5, 9–10, 12–15, 17–20, 22–24, 26–31, 33–35, 37–40, 42–44, 49, 52–58, 60–62, 64, 67–68, 72–73, 75–76, 78–85, 87

Cocoa powder, 51, 83

Coconut, 3, 5, 15, 19–21, 82, 84–85, 89

Coconut cream, 20

Coconut milk, 19–20, 82

Coffee, 4, 13, 17, 23, 49, 51, 66

Coffee liqueur, 17, 49, 51

Cola, 12, 14, 21, 29, 32–33, 39–40, 52, 56, 78–79, 81

Condensed milk, 27, 32–33, 40, 73–74

Coriander, 67

Crackers, 27

Cranberry, 5, 17–18, 58, 73, 77

Cranberry juice, 17–18, 58, 73

Rice, 72, 77

Rice wine, 77

Rosemary, 55

Rum, 10, 12, 14–15, 19, 21–23, 29–30, 32–33, 39–40, 52, 54–57, 78–79, 81, 84–85

S

Salad, 24

Salsa, 3–4, 31, 49–50, 65–66, 72

Salt, 8–9, 11, 16–17, 19, 22–31, 34–36, 38–40, 42–51, 53–55, 58–61, 63–70, 72, 74–75,

   77–86, 88–89

Savory, 49

Scallop, 49–50, 74

Sea salt, 31, 67

Seafood, 4, 49–50, 74

Seasoning, 48, 67, 85–86

Seeds, 25, 37, 50, 53, 56–57, 62, 65, 70, 82, 87

Shallot, 49

Soda, 9, 15, 18, 20, 22, 30–31, 35, 44–46, 51, 53–54, 56, 63, 68, 70, 72–73, 75, 77, 80,

   84–86, 89

Soup, 67

Spinach, 6

Steak, 66

Strawberry, 3–5, 11, 18, 22, 27, 40–41, 69–71, 85–86

Sugar, 8, 11–12, 18–19, 21, 24–31, 33, 35–38, 40–41, 43–64, 66–67, 69–71, 73–77, 82,

   85–87, 89

Syrup, 9–10, 13, 15, 19, 22, 25–26, 30–31, 34–35, 37, 40, 42, 55, 57–60, 63, 67, 73, 76–77,

   81–82, 85, 87–88

T

Tabasco, 72

Taco, 5, 72, 77

Tamarind, 76–77

Tangerine, 9, 41

Tea, 3–5, 8, 12, 14–15, 21, 30, 32–33, 39–40, 52, 56, 58, 78–79, 81

Tequila, 1, 3–6, 8–89

Thyme, 48

Tomato, 17–18, 72

Tomato juice, 17, 72

V

Vanilla extract, 40

Vegetable oil, 43, 66, 74

Vegetables, 6

Vermouth, 37, 78

Vinegar, 52, 57–58, 77–78

Vodka, 10, 12, 14–15, 19, 21–22, 29–30, 32–33, 39–40, 52, 54–56, 59, 78–79, 81, 84–85, 87

W

Watermelon, 3–5, 22, 35, 48, 62, 67–69, 86–88

Whisky, 85

White pepper, 67

White sugar, 8, 18, 21, 28, 30, 33, 35, 41, 44, 46–47, 51, 56, 61–63, 69, 86

Conclusion

Thank you again for downloading this book!

I hope you enjoyed reading about my book!

If you enjoyed this book, please take the time to share your thoughts and post a review on Amazon. It'd be greatly appreciated!

Write me an honest review about the book – I truly value your opinion and thoughts and I will incorporate them into my next book, which is already underway.

Thank you!

If you have any questions, **feel free to contact at:** _msdrink@mrandmscooking.com_

Ms. Drink

www.MrandMsCooking.com

Your Note

Your Note

Your Note

Your Note

Your Note

Your Note

Your Note

Your Note

Your Note

Your Note

Your Note

Your Note

Your Note

Printed in Great Britain
by Amazon